Chloe Shorten is a communications specialist, Queensland girl, mother of three and an advocate for improving the lives of women, children and people with disabilities. She lives in Melbourne and is married to Bill.

TAKE HEART

Chloe Shorten

a story for modern stepfamilies

MELBOURNE
UNIVERSITY
PRESS

For our dear children
Rupert, Georgette and Clementine

MELBOURNE UNIVERSITY PRESS
An imprint of Melbourne University Publishing Limited
Level 1, 715 Swanston Street, Carlton, Victoria 3053, Australia
mup-info@unimelb.edu.au
www.mup.com.au

First published 2017
Text © Chloe Shorten, 2017
Design and typography © Melbourne University Publishing Limited, 2017

The poem 'Children learn what they live' on p. 147 © 1972 by Dorothy Law Nolte.

Cover design by Clare O'Loughlin
Typeset in 12/16.5pt Bembo by Cannon Typesetting
Printed in Australia by McPherson's Printing Group

Cataloguing-in-Publication data for this title is available from the National Library of Australia

ISBN 9780522871326 (pbk)
ISBN 9780522871333 (ebook)

Contents

The book I wanted to read

WHEN I DECIDED to remarry and bring a stepfather into my children's lives, I needed to 'get it right'. I owed that to my kids.

I consulted experts for high-quality advice. I asked people I knew how they did it. There was a great bookstore in Brisbane opposite my office, and I scoured its shelves for stories of 'successful' outcomes for stepfamilies and particularly for the children involved. There are so many stepfamilies in history, with empires and monarchies built on remarriages! Completely head over heels and about to marry again, I wanted to show myself, my family and even my former husband it would all be okay. But the books I found were either instructive 'how to' ones that didn't include success stories or had titles along the lines of *Help! Yikes! We Are a Stepfamily* or *I'm No Stepmonster* that frightened me off. Later on, I would spend an entire day in a massive Barnes & Noble store in

New York—arguably a mecca for self-help, how-to and relationship advice books. But, again, what I really wanted wasn't there. Searching online bookstores wasn't very uplifting either. Meanwhile, it struck me that the media portrayed stepfamily situations unrealistically, with evil step-parents permeating TV shows and magazine articles.

I wanted to alleviate my anxiety, to empower myself with validating tales of the diverse and wonderful families I firmly believed ours could be. I knew we weren't alone, because in my quest I read all the research I could find. In Australia's population of 24 million people, there are around 5.7 million families with children and 2.8 million of these include kids under eighteen. A whopping 43 per cent of the kids under thirteen have experienced living outside the typical nuclear-family structure (Baxter, 2016a).

These are children in stepfamilies, and in lone-parent families. Many of these are shared-care families, where the children might live primarily with one parent but spend time with their other parent; or may be one of the small, but growing, number of families where children spend roughly equal time with each parent after a divorce. There are same-sex-couple families, and children living with grandparents or other relatives. So, modern Australian families are a tremendous mix. As the great chronicler of family life in this country, the Australian Institute of Family Studies (AIFS), found in October 2016, more than two in five Australian children experience living in families who don't fit the stereotype of Mum, Dad and a brother or sister.

Research shows the majority of kids do well in these environments, and for some, the change in their family life is of great benefit. While I think it's important to acknowledge the value of growing up in stable nuclear families, it is also crucial to be positive towards, and supportive of, those who are part of what academic lingo now calls 'complex families'. While I think that term is useful for research purposes, I just call these families 'the new normal'.

I needed to see stepfamily life in all its permutations and not through the lens of how a nuclear family evolves. I longed for long-term studies that showed how stepfamilies who 'do well' did it; I wanted to soak up joyful, moving and funny stories I could use as a model, and that would reassure the children and me, and enlighten and encourage my new husband, Bill Shorten, who was then a member of the Australian parliament. I wanted stories showing that with effort and the right kind of environment, kids in these sorts of very modern families actually thrive.

It was in the absence of instructive tales about, and models of, healthy stepfamilies that I turned to the research. The complexity of some family structures, the number of households involved, and the reluctance of some to identify as being in stepfamilies or to disclose any details means that real data is hard to get. The 2013 *Family Characteristics* report taken from the Australian census clearly warns its stepfamily statistics have 25–50 per cent unreliability for these reasons. So, the bulk of the long-term literature on stepfamilies is largely authored overseas, the accounts are often based on deficits and pathologies, and the figures are easy to misinterpret. As a career researcher and a big believer in evidence-based decision-making, I was gobsmacked. How can we, as a society, possibly be making good decisions, and creating good policies, services and support systems, for a huge and growing number of Australian families?

Relief came when I discovered new research that academics, clinicians and practitioners from the US, Australia, New Zealand, Canada and the UK have painstakingly undertaken. I have now read hundreds of academic papers, articles, books, speeches and editorials, and spoken to experts everywhere. Happily, in all this I found the most extensive examination of Australian stepfamilies ever undertaken. *Growing Up In Australia: The Longitudinal Study of Australian Children* looks at 8000 children from all states and territories whose lives researchers have focused on for more than a decade.

Also, demographer and senior research fellow Dr Jennifer Baxter's work for the AIFS is based on the longest-term analysis of the largest number of Australian families ever undertaken. Her report *Diversity, Complexity and Change in Children's Households* was released just as I started writing this book, with the AIFS saying, 'The [Baxter] study showed that a significant number of children live in more complex households, with the potential for this to impact both positively and negatively.'

All this has convinced me even more that not just interested parents like me but the whole community need to talk more about valuing families in all their wonderful complexity. As society changes, so do families, and we need to agree that different sizes and types of families are okay (and inevitable). We need broad understanding that the health of these microsystems is vital to our national wellbeing. That it's what we do within those families, how we learn from the lessons of the past and the researchers' toil that matters. That if we understand the imperative of consistent care, and a broad support network for children and parents, a warm, strong parenting method, and a community that doesn't judge and a system that supports them, then the kids will be all right.

I'd love to see all families have a greater share of the bandwidth in our public conversation.

The book I was searching for wasn't there and so this is why I decided to tell my story. But it's also the story of all those families who opened their hearts to me, and of the marvellous professionals who have unlocked the insights that modern Australian families need.

1

Mine is a modern Australian family

A S A GIRL, I had very fixed notions of my future. I would grow up, go to university, fall in love and get married, work and have children who would be like me. On the bus or in my bedroom, I named all the members of my family, including my husband. I would keep living in Brisbane, close to my family, and know just what to do as a spouse and parent.

In my ideal family, we would embrace all the traditions I grew up with, the milestones of life: celebrating birthdays, christenings, marriages and funerals, Christmas, Easter and family holidays. We'd watch movies together. My husband and I would watch from the sidelines at sports matches, and closely supervise homework, like my parents did with me and my siblings, Jack, Revy, Rupert and Tom. Education and being part of the community would be important, as would be sharing with my children a love of books and the arts, as my parents shared this with me.

I was very, very lucky that I had parents who were happy with, and lovely to, each other. They are very grounded people, and their marriage has lots of jokes and lots of warmth. They have been married fifty-four years, and many of their closest friends are celebrating similar grand anniversaries. All the families I grew up around were rather traditional, with lots of kids, which meant plenty of noise and activity. One of the things that worked for Mum and Dad was that they are good at problem solving: it's not that they didn't go through difficult times, but they navigated adversity together.

While I was growing up, my father had an architecture and design practice where, for over four decades, he employed hundreds of professionals of all ages, many of whom were parents. My brothers and sister and I spent quite a bit of time playing under his drafting table and it certainly was an early example of a flexible workplace. His practice eventually merged with an international firm, and this took him all over the world, advising on the built environment and corporate identity. Mum worked part time until we were in our teens, lecturing in law. At high school, I was one of the odd ones out in having a mother who worked full time.

So, I expected to replicate with my own family a childhood that was happy and pretty conventional, except that for my parents gender-based roles were less rigid because they had demanding careers. Dad was very much ahead of his time—he did a lot more of the hands-on parenting, the cooking, driving kids around and shopping, than did many men of his era.

I expected that my marriage would be a fairly equal partnership; that I would work and have my own life but still be a partner in a very solid unit. I had quite 'modern' views but also the traditional goal of having a close family like the one I grew up with.

And this is what I did. I met my first husband when I was twenty-one, at a friend's party, and married him at twenty-seven, though I had my first child later than I expected to, at twenty-nine. My first husband and I were together for sixteen years, until I was thirty-seven. My marriage ending was not easy for me. I felt like I had failed. It was very painful for all of us, my children, family, friends and their dad. It was not like celebrity divorces that make it look emotional but fairly simple. I don't think they are ever like that. By then, we had two children, aged six and seven, and they experienced the stages of grief as though a family member had died. Because, really, part of the family had.

My first husband is a talented architect, like my father. He had been married previously to a successful woman and had the view that women could do anything men could do. Still, it was tricky when I was trying to juggle my career in corporate communications, his ambitions, and two children under eighteen months. We worked hard to prevent the breakdown of our marriage, and it took a long time for our relationship to unwind. I suspect when we entered counselling, we did so a little too late.

It would have helped to know then what I know now: that, contrary to what I grew up with, long marriages are not a given. Marriage has been evolving throughout human history. In, for example, Old-Testament times, life expectancy was less than fifty, and marriage was largely for economic reasons and certainly not based on love—which is why Jesus' teaching about loving your wife or husband-to-be was quite radical. But modern life expectancy and its consequently elongated marriages have not really changed the idea of what a 'normal' family is.

There are many people living in healthy and strong family units who feel some groups in society see them as 'other'. For them to be regarded as 'other' simply doesn't reflect reality, or acknowledge that the idea of family is nothing if not dynamic.

In a similar time span to that of my first marriage, for instance, the number of people in the US who were married trended down from 70 per cent to just under 50 per cent. Currently, a third of Australian families are stepfamilies, and many more are sole-parent families, or shared-care families where there are two separated 'sole' parents, and the children spend time with each. The latest available data tells us that 72 per cent of Australian families with a child under eighteen are 'intact', or original-marriage, families. So, 28 per cent of families are those in which parents have separated or divorced, or in which children live with a sole parent from the start, or with same-sex parents, or with parents in a subsequent long-term relationship, either or both of whom have children from previous relationships.

Even the 2013 National Centre for Social and Economic Modelling (NATSEM) report *Modern Family* stated: 'Marriages were once the cornerstone of Australian families but over the past few decades Australian families have undergone significant change'. Yet, we're still hooked on marriage as the key way to define what a family is.

Before I learned about the huge variety and vibrancy of 'different', or non-nuclear, families in Australia, I felt like I lost part of my identity when my first marriage ended. I had a definite sense of failure that prompted a period of looking really hard at myself and the world around me. I saw divorce as the end of my family unit, and felt it keenly, especially because of the children. I think divorce is still regarded differently if there are children involved. I was certainly aware of this, in part because mine played out in the public eye but also because I was the first of my generation in the family to get divorced. When I looked into the family records, though, there was a great-great-grandfather, a cousin, and an aunt or two who had got divorced, just as there would be in most family histories.

Across all societies and cultures, family is still considered to be at the heart of society, the building block, a fundamental and universal element of all communities, despite the culture war over what 'true' family is. In Australia, we are experiencing a social revolution in types of families, but there needs to be more discussion about, and recognition of, this. It is a revolution among those who have formed families through circumstances, kinship and moral responsibility, not just through biology. Why aren't we being the supportive and encouraging community they need?

But, no matter what a family looks like, the work of parenting is still the same; it is the effort involved in providing a safe and happy home for children raised, with love and care, to maturity. It is in our collective interest for Australia's neighbourhoods to recognise, understand, encourage and support the wellbeing of all families. We need to tell and hear these households' stories without stigma or judgment.

I was surprised to learn that if you have kids, society looks at you differently once you are no longer married. This made me more self-conscious. For example, before I was divorced, I was a professional woman with children and did not see that as anything unusual, but after my first husband and I separated, I became more self-conscious about being a working mother and having the children with me most of the time (as if having a working single mother were viewed as a potential disadvantage for children, when having a working married mother wasn't). In hindsight, I realise this self-consciousness was due to my internal censor.

For the last two decades, I have worked as a communications specialist in large companies, specifically in the tech and resources sectors. This has brought me in contact with thousands of people all over Australia, many of whom worked in country towns, from the top of Queensland, to the Pilbara, to Perth and to Northern

Tasmania. I am drawn to regional towns, and loved being able to go to Rockhampton, Gladstone, Mackay, Cairns, Townsville, Launceston, Newcastle, Wollongong, the Fingal Valley, Devonport. I've relished working with skilled and interesting people in dynamic industries in an era of change and massive growth in Australia.

I've been very, very lucky to work for four CEOs, all men, who have been generous mentors and champions of women's equality. All of them fathers, interestingly; all with daughters. I spent a lot of time talking with people about their views and their families. From safety to training, from merging company brands to managing relationships with community groups and the media, and, some-times, preparing people for changes such as plant closures or new, higher-risk, projects. Some such changes are speedy and some move like glaciers. In any case, one of the most interesting parts of the job was working with communities and the workforce to create change, often bringing me in touch with mothers, wives and leaders of small communities. I learned very quickly that the key to productivity and safety in industrial environments was healthy and happy family lives for every employee. I met with the wives and partners of employees to seek advice about operational or shift changes, about safety initiatives, and mergers and acquisitions. I've never altered my view that supporting its families makes for a much healthier company.

Bill and I met through work, when he and I were speaking at a resources industry conference. As the head of the Australian Workers' Union, he was the headline act, talking to hundreds; and I was off-off-Broadway, in a steering group.

Listening with my boss to his address about people and work in the future, I agreed with his central premise but felt he hadn't made enough of the importance of women's emergence in the workforce, and, afterward, I told him.

The following year, our paths crossed again when he was travelling to mining and manufacturing sites to talk to union members about government policies and I was working for Australia's largest manufacturer of cement. Bill had become very well known in Australia as a union leader in 2006, when the Beaconsfield mine collapsed and two men were trapped and another killed. He became the conduit between the people on the ground and the rest of the country, who were watching it unfold on their TVs.

I had been doing a management course in Europe during that time, so I hadn't followed the mine collapse. I was asked to attend a site meeting, as media were travelling with Bill and part of my job was managing the company's relationships with the press. I knew little about unions but knew quite a bit about our workforce, their families and the pressures they faced. Instead of preventing Bill from coming into the manufacturing-site car park for a public televised meeting, I suggested to the operations manager that he invite Bill and his colleagues to the conference room to meet with our manufacturing workforce, many of whom were members of his union. It seemed the more enlightened way for them to engage. In the meeting, they talked about workers' rights and carbon pollution. (Not much has changed in those debates since.)

I was in the slow and difficult process of separation from my first husband, and it was a very stressful time for my family. My children and I moved into a place a few streets away from the family home. They went back and forth but mostly were with me, being so young. It was very important to me that they were connected to their dad. We lived like this for almost a year and a half before I decided my future was with Bill.

Living through that period was tough for all of us. The pain, loss, disruption, the difficulty for the children; trying to live in two homes, the economic losses. And living it through the lens of a camera was a particular trial. I wonder if the public nature of my divorce and remarriage compounded the anxiety I felt. But this also led me to think the stigma associated with, and stereotyping of, remarriage might hinder the establishment, strength and wellbeing of blended families, and was when I started scouring academic journals. Looking back, I think it was this that gave me the courage to write about the topic.

Because my parents were so (comparatively) modern in their way of thinking, I was a bit naive about some of the assumptions, stereotypes and judgments associated with working motherhood, because it was the norm in my home, both growing up and while I was married. But when you go through the process of getting unmarried, and then marrying again, all your choices, including all your parenting choices, are under a lot of scrutiny, by others and yourself. It can be a bit of a shock to the system to feel you suddenly have to explain yourself and your decisions to everyone around you—counsellors, lawyers and other outsiders. While you might be doing a great job as a married mother, you're doing it unobserved, but when you separate, you become more conscious of every little thing, even if nothing about your parenting has changed.

The upside for me was seeing what I could do better for my children, because everything became more magnified; it super-charged my motherhood like an electric shock. I became fierce and defensive about my mothering and my role as primary carer of my children. Because they were going through a major life transition, I became laser-focused. For a while, I was hyper-vigilant with mothering and probably overdoing it. But because I was made aware that what I was doing was outside the norm, I felt the need to compensate.

Another sign of just how strong are the underlying assumptions about what is the right and conventional family model is the high level of interest people have in someone else's separation. This was heightened, of course, in my case because the media reported on my personal life but it happens to a lesser, but no less real, extent to everyone. It's that kind of 'car crash' mentality that is hard-wired in us; that when we see an unexpected fate befall someone, part of us is compelled to look. Rather than us just being gawkers, though, it becomes a matter of 'What can I learn to avoid it happening to me?'. While this is a self-preservation instinct, it puts pressure on the family under scrutiny and can add to its isolation at a time when the community ought to protect it. Again, there were no easily available resources to help prepare me for this.

I'm not a clinician or a stepfamily researcher, so my contribution is my personal—deeply personal—experience. I'm making it only because I want to talk about the children in these common if 'unorthodox' family situations and promote their welfare and wellbeing.

Since becoming part of a stepfamily, I've felt deeply some of the intense bias against, and stereotyping of, these family arrangements, as I've met and talked with mothers and fathers around the country. Old myths and fairytales about 'wicked' step-parents still cast a shadow over the chances of success for people entering second marriages. I believe there is a tendency to view families formed by second marriages and involving children as 'less than' families consisting of married parents raising their own biological children. This can make those families seem more vulnerable. We musn't squander any more time on the myth that second families, or other non-nuclear groups, have any less claim to the word 'family' and all it stands for.

The risk of second marriages ending in divorce is already higher than that of first marriages, and, coupled with the increased pressure in the contemporary parenting atmosphere, it is important that non-nuclear families are embraced under the umbrella of 'family' comprehensively and for who they are, not for what they are perceived to lack. It seems ridiculous that the dominance of the idea the nuclear family is the 'true' way a family should be leaves out a third of the population.

That people in non-nuclear families are aware they are failing, in the minds of some, to be 'normal' is evident in many ways. Many people living in a 'step' situation do not even identify as being part of a stepfamily for data collection purposes, which, having experienced some of the stigma involved in the seven years I've been living in one, I would put down to being reticent to adopt a label with potentially negative connotations.

According to the AIFS (2016):

> stepfamilies are often unrecognized or unacknowledged within society. In part, a negative image that leads to reluctance to identify as a stepfamily may perpetuate their under-representation. At the same time, the contemporary stepfamily has a complex structure, and members face a number of notable challenges that are difficult to overlook.

The social mores, laws and expectations that have developed as a result of the historical predominance of the nuclear family have been useful but, with an increasing number of children living in other types of families, we need to acknowledge this reality in our dialogue, our policies and our attitudes. It's in all of our interests to recognise, understand, encourage and support all families, telling their stories without judgment.

The standards established by the rise of the nuclear family after the industrial revolution, such as how children should be treated, and about parental responsibility, were valuable. They also created social norms about the value of family in communities and how we should behave towards each other. From that came laws and a whole range of other measures to protect families, and that's a good thing and something we need to retain. But we also need to evolve, so as not to exclude other groups, those who can already be vulnerable just because they are beginning a family again, or doing it 'differently'.

In my exhaustive quest for useful information about ways to make 'unconventional' families thrive, I've realised things have been changing so fast that even the bulk of social research and social work theory is running behind reality, with family psychology clinical practitioners struggling to keep up. Just as I wanted to read stories that would reassure me my new family would have the same chance to thrive as others, and not be viewed as something less authentic or damaged per se, I want other parents to benefit from my learning and, especially, to understand that the first requirement when change happens is to be kind to yourself. Be aware that you will try to overcompensate for a turn in the family's path, whether you are becoming part of a stepfamily or a blended family, embarking on having a baby alone or engaging in any other variation on the nuclear-family structure.

Know that while some people will be disapproving, and shock you with their views and biases, others will pleasantly surprise you with their understanding, empathy and kindness. Surround yourself with people who are ready to have enriching conversations with you; those who leave you emboldened, pleasantly surprised and empowered, not those who will leave you bruised. Even though it can be excruciating, draw on your emotional intelligence and resilience in deciding 'Actually, I really don't need that person around me, it's just not helpful', and edit out people who have a destructive perspective on your life at an already challenging time.

When you are telling people about the imminent changes in your life, lower your expectations, no matter who it is: a sibling, a parent, your boss, your child's teacher or your GP. Too often, they can make the issue all about them. The ones who understand that what is happening is not about them will shine. You have to go through that tunnel of having those conversations, and remember that you are resolute, you are doing your best and it's going to be okay.

It's a time when you need to hear stories from other people who have been through the same experience, and can reassure you that the kids will be all right if you work through everything well. Expert resources are also helpful. We started seeing a family psychologist whom we continued to consult over the years and whose sturdy support became invaluable.

Luckily, I had wonderful friends, from my best mates, to women in my mothers' group. I had lots of resources and support, which is one reason I felt compelled to share my story. If you don't hear from people who say, 'This has happened to me and this is how I have done things, and so far, so good,' then how are you going to know what might happen?

Even much of the published self-help material comes from the perspective of 'You're a little bit broken and we've got to fix you', as opposed to 'You're moving on, and need to put your best foot forward', and showing that there is even something lovely about the experience. There will be pain involved, but in the wound lies the gift.

Professor Paul Amato, a worldwide authority on stepfamilies and based in the US, has written a lot on the subject of how kids really fare after divorce and remarriage, and has drawn a picture of the overall outcomes for families, the good and the bad. His many studies support what is now the accepted wisdom of experts in the field: that children can and do do well, and some even show an improvement in behaviour, after their parents divorce. In the 1990s, he looked at how kids in stepfamilies who thrived differed from those who suffered. Despite the diversity in stepfamily models, he argues, the outcome for children boils down to two main things: managing resources and stressors. If they have resources and don't have extra stressors, they have more opportunities and are protected from some of the adverse impacts of adjustment. Amato (1993) wrote:

> Major resources for children include parental support (emotional support, practical help, guidance, supervision and role models) as well as parental socioeconomic resources. Children with high levels of resources not only have opportunities to develop social and cognitive forms of competence, but are better able to deal with stressful life situations than are other children.

Stressors include the inter-parental conflict that may precede and follow divorce, as well as subsequent disruptive life changes. So, minimising stressful changes and events has a protective benefit for the kids, yet few of us go through this stage with enough awareness of such findings, which was another inspiration for this book.

How Australian families look in 2016 is part of the largest demographic change in the modern history of family life. It is an extraordinary revolution, in which a huge variety of 'new' family forms are becoming mainstream, but we have, as yet, too few public role models. Because we all do know of great functioning families in different family forms.

2

A new normal

FOR ANYONE WHO divorces, there is, for the children and the spouses, a period of mourning and feeling vulnerable, and there certainly was for me. In both my personal and my professional life, I was careful who I spoke to about what I was going through. But, in the midst of me helping my little children and our extended families to adjust, there were newspaper headlines announcing to the whole country my new relationship (and, no, much of what was reported wasn't accurate). This was not lost on the people swirling around me in daily life, at the school drop off, in the corridors of my office, or at the local shops. Some would argue the intrusion was part of the rough and tumble of public life, but I wasn't then in public life and nor were the kids.

But while I wasn't always a public figure, I am the daughter of public figures. My mother had been appointed governor-general of Australia. It was unique in the history of the Commonwealth that the head of state's representative had a son-in-law serving the parliament. Separation and divorce are never a picnic but doing it in the public eye was blast-furnace-level character building.

The children's dad agreed to me having them live with me in Melbourne. All of us—me, their dad and Bill—were focused on making sure they had as much support as possible during their transition. With this aim, Bill and I saw our brilliant family counsellor every two weeks in the period leading up to the move from my then home in Brisbane to our new home in Melbourne. In his modest and kid-friendly rooms near a Brisbane hospital, Bill and I would talk through our plans and discuss the kids' wellbeing. A congenial and very experienced child psychologist, with decades of experience helping kids through trauma, he was straight-talking and put us at ease with dad jokes. He was the perfect teacher for us.

The children were bright and beautiful, and much loved by their parents, family, friends and neighbours. We talked about how it was important to give Rupert (then aged seven) and Georgette, or Gigi, (then aged six) space to be sad about what was no longer and what was changing. It's about helping kids understand they don't have to be instantly bonded and loving to the new person in your life; that fostering respect and friendship is what's important. In our case, they had a father but also had someone they might want to see as another father figure.

The children's father would see them regularly and during school holidays, and we'd fly them up to see him or he would fly down to Melbourne, which he did regularly for work. Our little girl was at an age where dollhouses and dressing up were the thing, and Rupert was into the super-cool little boy fad of Yu-Gi-Oh! cards, cartoons and superheroes. The move from Queensland to Victoria felt like we were migrating to another country. While the kids were on holidays with their dad at the beach, I packed up everything—each book, stick of furniture, CD and toy—and put them all on a truck, and then put my car on a train.

I arrived in Melbourne in the dear old suburb of Moonee Ponds, bang between the airport and the city, walked into the house Bill and I had bought (with the children's 'help' as we looked at real estate websites) and listened to the sound of kids in a nearby playground. The removal truck arrived, and as the movers unpacked, the lady from the house across the road walked over to scold them about letting me lift anything, because she could see I was (very happily) pregnant. She introduced herself to me in a thick Italian accent as Giusepina and went to get me some Italian bread.

It came to light over the following days that Giusepina had migrated to Melbourne, from Italy, with four little children. She had made the trip alone, with her husband having come earlier, and she knew no one else in Melbourne. She had started again, much like me. I've come to love Giusepina—with whom I share a birthday—like an aunt; the kids call her Nonna and my friends adore her. We know well, and admire, her adult children and grandchildren, and share celebrations and milestones. I didn't set out actively to recruit her as part of my new life but, having found each other, we formed such a strong bond. Our bond with Giusepina, and with other people living near us, was an essential part of building the stable network we wanted to create for our children.

As soon as they arrived, the kids started decorating their bedrooms. They went off to Ikea with Bill, and chose their colours, chairs, lamps and beanbags; found easels and art tables, basketball hoops and ballgames. From early on they seemed to be adjusting well, and, due to their outgoing personalities, were open to meeting new people and making new friends. I watched them like a hawk—sometimes too closely—keeping a careful eye out for any sign, not matter how tiny, that something was upsetting them and needed to be worked through steadily.

A lot of parents will find that they are time poor and they will often be working full time in the years after a separation, which poses a problem, given the increased time and attention the kids will need. I continued to work full time, as head of communications at one of the large resources companies in the country, and negotiated flexible arrangements with my employer so I could be with the children as much as possible. I reduced as much as possible any time spent away from them in the evenings or at weekends. I pared back other commitments, and some people stopped asking me to do things after a while. Though I found this a bit isolating, I adjusted, and had friends and family visit, to provide contact, support and continuity.

The aggregation of all the research I unearthed suggested children do best after their parent separates in the following circumstances (which I call 'If's): if they are still in touch with the parent they aren't living with; if they aren't exposed to conflict between their parents, including being caught in the middle of it; if they haven't suffered economic deprivation or hardship after the separation; and if they aren't dealing with other stressful life events or situations.

Having learned that poor outcomes in behaviour, academic achievement and self-esteem are related to a lack of investment and supervision by parents, I sought ways of increasing my contact with, commitment to and communication with the kids. I would leave housework or office-related work until after they were asleep, so I could be around, sorting their bookshelves, or hovering in the corridor in case they started a conversation. It was a good ploy, as they would usually want a chat.

The amount of time, attention and the quality of parenting children receive especially in the first few years of adjustment has been found to make a big difference. There is a growing body of evidence about the impact on children of living in a hostile family environment. Whether it's a result of parental conflict, disengaged or neglectful parenting, or other factors, the children may have long-term problems as a result. This is the case in nuclear families as well as other types of families. I read studies by psychiatrists, psychologists, sociologists and other experts about what leads to divorce and what leads to remarriage, among other parental decisions. I found the arguments in support of preventing separation at all costs were weak, and that the effort should be expended on preventing discord in the first place. However, given that the toothpaste is not going to go back into the tube for some people, I examined the impact on children whose parents stayed together with high levels of discord, conflict or lack of cooperation. What I found was bleak.

Paul Amato and fellow US expert Joan Kelly have undertaken exhaustive studies on how children cope after divorce. They found that while there is a lot known about the impact of divorce on children, there is insufficient attention paid to the damaging impact on them of highly troubled marriages: 'Children living in marriages with frequent and intense conflict are significantly more likely to have substantial adjustment problems before parental divorce and compromised parent-child relationships' and 'These findings suggest that the deleterious effects of divorce have been overstated.' Engaging and supporting parents in the relationship and preventing the problems would lower the number of kids experiencing the fallout of their parents' poor relationships. In 2005, Amato examined families in the US, and how kids in stable families with two parents who were married to each other did compared with other children. He looked at marriage-promotion policies and how they affect kids' wellbeing, and found that interventions affect it only modestly 'because children's social and emotional problems have many causes, of which family structure is but one' but that even a small decrease in the percentage of marriages ending in divorce is of substantial social benefit. However, if a separation occurs and stepfamilies are formed, they have to develop the skills that all families should use for committed and conscious parenting.

I recently asked Georgette, who is now a strong and straightforward young lady, how she felt about that time of transition in her life. Interestingly, many of her comments revolved around how she felt about her bedroom: 'When I first moved here, my room was spotless and didn't feel homey. It was unfamiliar, and felt forced and new and a bit stressful,' she told me. 'Lovely paper lanterns were hung in my room all over the ceiling—Bill and a friend put them there to surprise me.

'I also started at dance school, which was my little place too. I was still coming to terms with a new person in my life, and slowly came to realise he was an extra parent and not trying to replace Dad.

'When I went away, you always did something nice for me in my room, like an improvement, but it meant it was unfamiliar again when I got back. I've customised my room and my environment is my own now. With my interests and passions, every little detail is mine.

'I loved family movie night and UNO cards, and having a fireplace, so there were marshmallows to roast. I had two giant teddies from Bill. One in Brisbane, Rosie, and it was a comfort symbol. The next one, Posey, I got from Bill when Clemmie was born; I still have them in my room.

'A big thing was going to select our dog; it was a great day. The litter was so cute, and we took home Theodore, driving really slow in the car, so we didn't scare him in his puppy house.

'I also remember my first day in the new school when I was six, sitting in for a few hours. I was quite nervous, and I wore a yellow top and pink shorts. I made friends that day and two ended up being in my class. Sometimes I would feel new and lonely, but by the time I was in grade three, I found my people, my little gang of friends. I was fancy-free and happy.'

While Bill was doing his utmost, his routines were very work orientated, and cooking and planning ahead for domestic matters were not things he brought to the relationship. It was an adjustment for him that he needed to do family-type grocery shopping. I remember him going out to buy food for the weekend, and that when he came back what he'd bought consisted of Weet-Bix, ham, cheese, bread, hummus, mineral water, pasta and some onions. And dishwashing tablets. During dinner recently, I told the kids about it and they laughed heartily, and teased Bill for thinking that would be enough. They also defended him, though, because at that stage he was 'still on training wheels'.

As we all settled in, I continued to devour all the research I could get my hands on, knowing, as does anyone who has entered into a 'step' or 'blended' family, that bringing in a new person, even one the children trusted, carried enormous hopes and expectations, and was a big ask for everyone. I discovered a frustrating lack of statistical information about non-nuclear families, which, in part, has been put down to many people living in stepfamilies, or other non-traditional family models, being loath to identify themselves as such due to lingering negative connotations—the existence of which no one seems able to explain.

The number of these families is hard for statisticians to estimate because the census only collects data on 'the number of persons usually resident in the same household'. This means those stats underestimate the numbers, and fail to distinguish households where children live part time or where the non-resident parent has repartnered, so only one household is counted (Qu and Weston, 2005).

Most stepfamily researchers estimate that it takes anywhere from three to five years for a family to re-stabilise following formation of a stepfamily. Yet, researchers often rely solely on data from newly formed stepfamilies, where challenges are more apparent, and do not analyse stabilised stepfamilies or the factors that contribute to their longevity (Hetherington, 1999).

There is also a lack of consistent language and definitions relating to stepfamilies, and our legal system needs to catch up with the Australian family's changing face. There are laws that make children and step-parents legal strangers to each other: in the event of a child being taken to hospital in an emergency, the step-parent can't approve a medical procedure, for example.

We need better information, including research, data, longitudinal results and analysis of what works, early intervention services and policies. We need more sensitivity from service providers, schools, hospitals, agencies, lawyers, health workers, counsellors and teachers. Because the stepfamily, the blended family, the sole-parent family and the same-sex-parent family have been considered aberrations for so long, they are still often treated as 'other', when it's way past time for them to be regarded as just plain 'us'.

Nearly one out of two children growing up in Australia today can expect to become part of the nation's divorce statistics: 43 per cent of marriages can be expected to end in separation within thirty years. In 2001, 53 400 Australian children under the age of eighteen experienced their parents divorcing. An unknown number of children experienced their cohabiting parents separating. Also in 2001, almost a million children had one of their natural parents not living with them.

The Australian Bureau of Statistics (ABS) projects that by 2036, Australia will be home to 9 016 900 families. Of these 1 537 008 will be sole-parent families, 3 624 756 million will be couples with children, and there will be 151 316 other types of families. Proportionally, stepfamilies make up 10 per cent of couples with children, so this would mean at least 360 000 stepfamilies.

The ABS has traditionally defined a 'blended family' as a family with a couple and at least two children, one of whom was born to both of the remarrying partners and one of whom is a stepchild of either member of the couple (this is technically our family, though I don't think families really 'blend' as such). A 'stepfamily' is a family with a couple in which there is at least one child who is a stepchild of either parent, but no child who is the natural offspring of both the partners.

The ABS says the increase in the number of blended families is the largest noticeable change, brought on by rising divorce rates and the tendency of people to 'stick it out' in unsuccessful marriages for some years before divorcing, and thus repartnering with children in tow. One third of registered marriages in Australia involve at least one previously divorced partner. That a large number of second marriages involving children can falter—60 per cent within the first five years—is a strong motivator for anyone in this situation to learn everything they can about how to boost the new unit's chances of survival.

As my pregnancy progressed, I kept scouring the internet (including the *Stepfamilies Australia* website and raisingchildren.net), bookstores and libraries. Luckily, I also had family friends and other contacts who could introduce me to experts in parenting and family matters, among them academics, researchers and practitioners. I was grateful for being so fortunate as to have these guides to help me navigate this new territory and conscious that not everyone does. Through my family lawyer, I was able to talk to an excellent expert in family psychology about divorce and starting a stepfamily: how you go about it, and what the likelihood was of success, or problems to watch for, and what the challenges were. I was not, in any way, romanticising what it would be like.

That said, I really had my eyes opened to the fact that the kind of myths and fantasies about stepfamilies I saw in the shows I watched as a kid were just that: mythical. There was *The Brady Bunch* (about a widower, a divorcee with a mystery ex who was never mentioned, and three kids each); *Eight Is Enough* (about a widower with eight children who marries again); and even *Family Affair* (about a bachelor and his butler raising three orphaned nieces and a nephew). All these showed parenting in such situations to be quite easy. So, much of what pop culture has had to say about stepfamilies is not just unrealistic, it's unhelpful, for the most part. The plot of the movie *Stepmom*, starring Susan Sarandon and Julia Roberts, for example, had ridiculous expectations of the mother-and-stepmother relationship. The concept that these two women would end up not only semi-coparenting but being best friends is really quite silly.

In contrast, through my research and family counselling, I learned to lower my expectations of how everyone would slot into their new place; that it would be hard work, that I needed to be patient, and that it takes time. Bringing a new person into a family, with the overlay of the other person having 'left' the original family, is not an instant process, and the roles are not the same as those in the nuclear-family model.

Getting an understanding of what everyone thinks and hopes is important—the earlier the better—and these conversations need to be had again and again, as things change and the children get older. I wish I'd sat the kids down early in the piece and asked them more questions: 'What do you think a stepfamily is?' and 'What do you think it should be?'. We had talks about the changes but, on reflection, I think I thought they were too young to discuss them in detail. But we do talk (and text) about these things now.

For both the children and the step-parent, it's a matter of trying to be flexible during what can be a tense time time where everyone is a little fragile. You need to say up-front, 'Listen, you're not expected to call this person Mum or Dad. You're not expected to instantly feel like you have to do everything they say. They're not a replacement parent—they're another kind of parent, and they can do Dad-like things or Mum-like things; they're there for you.' That takes some of the pressure off all the emotions that go along with becoming part of a stepfamily, which for children can include guilt that they are getting along so well with another person who's not their biological parent.

Unless there has been abuse, or something else causing them not to feel grief at the old family unit ending, children are still often lamenting, or grieving, its loss and that takes time. A way to approach it with them is that loss is part of the cycle of life. And it is a part that needs to be acknowledged.

Research says that, depending on the ages of children when their biological parents part, it can take around five years for that grieving to lift before they start to settle in and put down roots, and get a real sense of the new family unit. And that process includes helping them understand—if they are at least five years old or so, and therefore old enough to understand—that they are not responsible in any way for their parents' separation.

Again, there is no 'one size fits all' model of the 'normal' Australian family: that it contains two married parents of around the same age, with the same cultural background, and with married grandparents living nearby. We live in an era when even the circumstances of intact nuclear families vary so much: many people are having their first child much later than did previous generations; more people live far away from their extended family; people are marrying across faiths and cultures; advanced fertility treatment is giving couples who would previously never even have had the chance to start a family a path to parenthood through donor genetic material and surrogacy. The concept of family has never been more broad.

The upside of all the challenges involved in modern families is that while the early days of forming a new version of your family can be a tense and fragile time it can also be an incredible, wonderful time. It is mostly a hopeful and special period in the lives of the parents and, often, also in the lives of the children. There is a lot of joy to be had, but you need to understand that you are not replicating a nuclear family. And, with that, take heart, I say!

Traditions continue and roles remain in a new family, but who carries those roles out changes. And you establish a new history together by creating rituals. For us, a lot of them were based around cooking, eating and dinnertime, and new ways of checking in with how other people in the family were feeling. For us, no question is ever off the table; that was one of the important things, to say regularly, 'Look, do you have any questions?'

And even with traditions from the first family that you keep, things don't need to be exactly the same. Because our kids are very musical (six choirs, two bands, four instruments and ten musicals later), I joke with them that we're a bit like the Von Trapps—Maria von Trapp, of course, was a stepmother. Starting out on the path of being a new family is like saying, 'Let's start at the very beginning', and we'll each take a piece of it and then put the music together down the track. You need to know the melody and everybody has a role, and if you're not a baritone, you don't have to try to make yourself into a baritone ... Well, the musical metaphors work for us!

As I embarked on a path no one else of my generation in my family had trodden—breaking the nuclear-family mould—it dawned on me that, though I had thought nothing of it at the time, no fewer than three of my best friends, Louise, Sally and Caroline, were raised by their mothers alone. Each had capable, highly educated and professional mums. Each became an incredible, professional woman herself. As well, two of my childhood friends lived in stepfamilies. One was particularly close to her stepdad— indeed, for years I didn't realise he was her stepdad—the other was respectful of, even if not close to, her stepmother.

That said, in Brisbane in the 1970s the statistics were not as they are today. Most of our friends fitted a standard model. They lived in large, intact families who went to church on Sundays, which we often did too. That church gave me comfort during turbulent times in my life, right up to when I moved to Melbourne. I loved the fact that the lady who taught me religious studies at infant school was still a member of the church when we baptised Rupert and Georgette there.

The permanent welcome offered by my church, like the support of our wise GP and other pillars in our community, were things I took for granted. I didn't realise how important those parts of our landscape and history were until I left them. Even before I looked at real estate in Victoria, I was looking for a spiritual home in Melbourne. When life's recognisable touchstones are shifted, and so much upheaval is happening at once, establishing those connections feels terribly important. It's about connecting and grounding yourself and your newly reshaped family.

I was baptised and confirmed in the Anglican Church, studied for my confirmation, and took the church's lessons in being a couple before my first wedding, which a minister conducted on a beach off Fiji. Bill grew up Catholic, and his parents worked incredibly hard to put him and his twin brother through Xavier College to be educated in the Jesuit tradition. (He is still very thankful for their sacrifices.) It was important to me to marry Bill in my church. He understood this, having attended the church with me in St Lucia where I grew up. When I started to come to Melbourne to visit him, he took me to visit the local Anglican churches.

I settled on a little old bluestone church near our house, and then called on the couple who were in residence next door: the vicar and his wife. Part of a stepfamily themselves, they welcomed us, counselled us in the way only people who had merged their lives through remarriage could, and warmly embraced us. They have continued to be a generous presence in our lives even now that they have retired and moved away.

Because, like most of the men and women I grew up with, I'm a feminist, a few people have asked me why I remarried, instead of living de facto with Bill and the children. I did so because I'm also rather old school, in that I like marriage and, in particular, the stability it gives to children. I knew of the protective benefits stable relationships (including marriage) offer children, and I also wanted there to be a clear structural bond between the children and their new baby sister. Research from the US shows that children benefit from society formally recognising their parents' relationship, whether we agree or not that a particular status should be assigned to children with married parents. This is another reason I advocate for equal marriage; if there are thousands of children being raised by same-sex-couple parents in Australia, why should they not have the same privilege? The rights of the child should be paramount.

So, I suppose I'm a proponent of marriage but I'm certainly not judgmental towards those who don't get married. It is nobody's business but their own.

Perhaps I was a little naive about the likely level of attention that would come Bill's and my way. No one expects to have a helicopter hovering over their wedding, unless they're a celebrity. Or a fugitive. Ours was a celebration, and very sweet except for the need to have police there, and cameras pointing at my pregnancy bump. I loved my blush-coloured dress and, though I felt raw and vulnerable, I was deeply happy there was a baby coming, and the two little hands holding ours tightly at the church were attached to little people who were smiling too.

I was wobbly on my small heels and shaking a little when I took my beautiful father's arm for him to walk me down the aisle of the church, my little girl in front of me with her armful of flowers. As always, my father gave me stability. All the faces in the small church had warm and encouraging expressions. I looked ahead to see my glorious little son, taking the ceremony very seriously and holding Bill's hand.

3

Resilience— A pilgrim's progress

WHEN I WAS growing up, girls were told that it was best for women to aim to be 'E.M.P.': engaged, married, pregnant, in that order. It was never made clear to me why women were expected to do things in any particular order, who dictated it, or whose approval we were seeking by doing so. Still, I never questioned any of this until things in my own life did not go as I'd expected, planned or could have imagined. Then I started to question—a lot—the 'rules' around what 'the right' way to do family is.

I've now learned that it's the institutionalisation of the nuclear family in most modern cultures that gives us this EMP timeline. Australian social psychologist Judith Planitz (2009) says:

Research on stepfamily stereotypes has been dominated by one broad perspective; nuclear family ideology. This view is that biological families have roles and responsibilities by a predictable series of events. In contrast, stepfamilies and other types of family units, may not have this predictable series of events consequently parental roles are less clearly defined in stepfamilies.

Because stepfamilies are not recognised to be an institution, comparative norms, descriptors and even legal rights and responsibilities for them, simply don't exist.

In my experience, when you're a product of Australia's middle class, it's only when you make a serious diversion from what is considered 'the norm' that you have reason to question those underlying assumptions about how life should be lived. Just who are we so afraid of disappointing and how much does it really matter if we don't conform? Judging by the furore over something as obvious as same-sex couples being allowed to marry, it seems to matter a lot, and I still cannot understand why.

Eight years after my first child, Rupert, was born, I was more than 1500 kilometres away from him and his sister, having a baby when I was in a new marriage and a new home in a new town. I felt very brave and a little wild. And I was also frightened. I wondered what the baby—whom the kids wanted to call Popcorn—would mean for the little ones, and how we would all adjust to yet another change none of us could have expected even a few years earlier. Having a baby is an herculean thing; having a baby at the same time as undergoing so many other life changes felt Olympian.

A few days after her birth, we brought our tiny girl, wrapped like a spring roll, home and waited for Rupert and Georgette to arrive in Melbourne. The memory of those first, tentative hours waiting for my children to meet their new baby sister still sits close to my heart; wrapped up, like Clementine. I was anxious. I assumed they were too. They were getting a new sister, a stepfather, a new school, and a new home in one giant step. Bill went from having zero to three kids in one fell swoop. A family was assembled in a week and Baby Clementine felt like its golden thread.

Georgette said later that she was so excited, she remembers exactly where she was when I was giving birth. A typical teen, she recalls it this way: 'We were driving with Dad, going past Uncle David's farm, and I was freaked out; "I have a sister." When I got to our home in Melbourne, there she was, sleeping in the bassinet, and I wanted to grab her.

'I used to brush her fine hair; I would want to scratch off the cradle cap. Every now and then, I'd get jealous of the baby brat in the house but I got over that; I always loved her. She was a little presence all the time. She clung onto me while I walked round the house, but she's too big for that now. I loved taking her over to Nonna, who'd give us the best, ripest figs and Clemmie would say, "Dat'sa myyy figgi": "that's my fig" in a Sicilian accent. I was fascinated by her and now she is fascinated by me!'

I recently asked Clementine, 'What's it like being in a stepfamily?' and she simply said, 'What's that?' Even though the experts tell you children are adaptable, and a stable, happy home with plenty of love is their primary need, it's still easy to cling to your doubts that all this could possibly work out okay. But when you hear from your child's mouth that she doesn't even realise her family is not just 'a family' but has some kind of prefix, you know the reassuring research was right all along.

I think Gigi may initially have been a little put out when Baby Clementine 'stole' her position in the family, as she would have loved to remain the baby forever. I put this to her while writing this book, to which she replied, 'I thought that when I became a middle child, I'd be neglected like in the TV shows; but my ideas *were* informed by television.' See what I mean about pop culture setting what we come to think of as standards?

So, Gigi and Rupert loved their new sister immediately, and they have barely put her down in the last seven years. Sometimes, when we're feeling especially lucky to have her, we say we feel like the bell may ring and there'll be someone in Tibetan robes at the door to take away our little gift, as her presence can seem too good to be true.

However, because of Bill's public profile, while we were making all the new discoveries about life as a brand-new family, there was the added stress of living in the limelight. The kids not only had to adapt to a lot of changes, they were aware of the headlines about their mum and her new partner. Such headlines hollered: 'MP Bill Shorten expecting child with Chloe Bryce', 'Bill Shorten in love with Quentin Bryce's daughter', 'Baby Clementine wows Labor MP Bill Shorten'; even 'GG seeking advice over Shorten connection'. Apparently, our relationship was some kind of constitutional crisis for a few gossips. Obviously, we weathered this, but many more headlines would follow. Learning to deal with that as a family was part of building our resilience as a unit and as individuals within that cohesive whole.

Our Brisbane counsellor had told us to expect it to take about five years for the children really to put down roots in their new life. We trusted his guidance, and it anchored us. Because he stressed that forming community and neighbourhood connections is important to children, we worked very hard to find the right local school, home, street and neighbourhood. He advised us as well to establish a firm routine and rituals, which also make children feel safe and secure. We introduced new ones, like movie night on Fridays, and stories at bedtimes became sacrosanct. Bill would break appointments if necessary, or leave functions early, to get home to read to the kids *Horrible Histories* or *Tintin*, or Roald Dahl stories like *Charlie and the Chocolate Factory*.

Sure enough, almost five years to the date of the move, I sensed that the children had settled in and found a rhythm to their lives, despite the unusual element of growing up in the public gaze. Their sense of belonging, due to their routines, their knowledge of the neighbourhood and their friendships, helped make this happen. The sleepovers, movie nights at school, the teachers they liked, and joining everything and trying things out—soccer, tennis, ballet, language classes and lots of musical activities—each left a little footprint and some small connection.

I found my mother's words from her Boyer Lecture 'Back to Grassroots', about the importance of feeling part of a community and a neighbourhood, helpful:

> As a child, I loved to be included; it was fascinating and fun. But even then I could see there were deeper layers to it. These people were our friends, our neighbours, shopkeepers, farmers, shire counsellors, my parents' colleagues, the matron of the local hospital.
>
> In a small town, everyone pretty well knows everyone. You feel very strongly that you're part of something, together. In boom times and tough times.

Similarly, a study by the Australian Institute of Health and Welfare found: 'The school and community contexts in which children live also have a considerable influence over their health, development and wellbeing. These contexts, along with family, set foundations for learning, behaviour and health over the course of their life.'

As well as really knitting into the neighbourhood in this early stage of being a new family, we were helped by the advice to provide 'constancy', and to learn what our children, collectively and individually, liked doing. In the case of Rupert, aged seven, this meant Yu-Gi-Oh! cards, Uno, Bakugon and Pokémon. Bill, as are other stepfathers, was advised to learn the games Rupert liked and play them with him. (Bill still laughingly describes learning the Yu-Gi-Oh! rules as a 'Tolkienesque nightmare'.) This meant actively making a space for play and for participating in their lives, not just expecting them to participate in ours. This gives children a sense of having at least some power, even if they cannot control everything that's going on with them. Bill and Gigi, who share a grand passion for books, created their own little world: Planet BG (Bill and Gigi). In this landscape, I was apparently Planet Boring … but it was a delight, really. Having an open-plan kitchen and living space was also great, as we were, and still often are, all in together, reading, sharing music, playing charades or Monopoly; doing the stuff families do, no matter what label the 'EMP' rule makers may assign them.

I put a lot of energy into making connections at the kids' primary school, and tried to play matchmaker, *Fiddler on the Roof*–style, to help them find friends. I was constantly open to trying new things: bowling, Scouts and helping out at soup kitchens. (While Rupe was at Scouts, he was a little surprised to see his grandma's portrait on the hall wall.)

We got to know the history of the suburb, tales of the old houses and their place in gold rush history. While the houses around us are modest Victorian cottages, up on the hill are some grand old homes of the district. The children know about the waterways, migration and industry in our area, and we have even toured the Maribyrnong River on a little old boat to show them another perspective on it.

There were lots of plants that were new to the three of us: cherry blossoms and cooler-climate natives than we knew from our Queensland life. The sky was different—the light was different, more muted and mellow, less hot and sharp. And there was the shock of cold, quiet evenings after humming, humid nights in a Queenslander-style house.

I know I was earnestly diligent about the kids' routines; perhaps a little too much so. I was definitely more dedicated to routine than I had been the first time around, maybe because of feeling that, since they had been through plenty of changes, I needed to show them just how committed I was to making everything as smooth as possible for them. The temptation to overdo this is real and hard to resist.

During this time of starting to put down roots, or even just shoots of roots, it was probably a blessing that I was not working outside the home. As this was the case for the first time in six years, this felt like a change of identity. I had transformed from a busy corporate executive into a full-time wife and mother, whose main job was helping a new family to form. I threw myself into finding a family doctor (to my mind, a key safety net for any family), a childcare centre I could trust, a dentist, barbershop, pharmacy; the lot. Such was my need to have all this in place by the time the children moved permanently to Melbourne, four weeks after I did, everything was mapped out for them in advance. Bill checked in with me constantly, calling friends and the local connections we needed, and introducing me to people. While I was nervous, he was born for this kind of relationship building, which was lucky because, politics being what it is, we didn't always have the luxury of carrying out this vital stage of family building in private. Bill and I agreed with Rupert and Gigi's dad that we should do our utmost to keep them out of the Klieg lights of public life. (Of course, that was before they were old enough to get onto social media, when any control over this was suddenly gone.)

I'd been through losses and changes that not everyone can understand. I wasn't the same person. And I felt a sense of failure at the same time as I felt a great sense of wonder at, and gratitude for, my extraordinary new relationship. I sought out other stepfamilies and non-nuclear families, of whom there were some at the children's new primary school. When I was among non-'traditional' families, I felt the glare of judgment was dimmer.

For the first few years after the move and the arrival of the new baby, it continued to be my mission to help my children feel that they belong in their new school, in their new home. I participated in local events and went out of my way to meet people, to exchange kindnesses and vulnerabilities, so as to build our familiarity with the neighbourhood. We did a lot of walking with the pram, to parks and other places to play, and saying hello to people watering their garden, picking olives off trees or walking their dog.

Bill was friends with a marvellous family nearby who have lived there for years, and the lady of the house, Marlene, the grandma, is a great baker, stalwart and terribly funny, and taught my kids how to bake biscuits and sausage rolls—we still toot our horn every time we drive past her house. We met a scientist who lives nearby, who teaches Clementine words in Mandarin. I formed a grand friendship with a mum at the kids' school. We found a music teacher who has a baby grand piano in the living room, and plays jazz standards for my buddy and me to sing; she has a charming husband who's a chef and who makes soup for us if the children are sick.

Our neighbours have been invited to all our celebrations, and we cherish them; they've been glue sticking us to our new life. While I was quite shy at first, I wanted the kids to know the stories of the people around them. Now they know a gentleman in the next street who has lived in his house for seventy years, and to whom they tell jokes and ask questions. They know the groovy empty-nesters who walk by with their Scottish Terriers, and a Greek couple with little English to speak of but great big hearts— and lemons. Thank the Lord I met three very warm, funny women from my neighbourhood, who have been in that kitchen of mine ever since, our children's lives intertwined like new puppies.

Local events are important to us and, because Bill has the job he has, the kids have been cuddled by members of every ethnic and community group in Melbourne. It stands them in great stead; I know it makes them feel they belong. The children have been fearless, adventuresome and compassionate. I'm in awe of them.

As well as all this external bonding, we've worked on their sense of belonging inside the family. We told them stories of other families with new babies, and bought quantities of books about 'how to' and 'how not to' go about being a family. When I was diving into whatever research I could find about step and blended families, migrant families, children of divorce, children raised by grandparents and in foster families, or by same-sex-couple parents, I would report back to my own family. (I'd also remind the kids that Jesus had a stepdad, which just made them glare at me.) Sometimes my drive to unearth the ultimate explanation and information about the family unit I was now in became almost all-consuming. This need to know may in part have been about reassuring myself that, despite the intrusive headlines, we were all doing fine.

While all this reading helped, I was surprised to learn that, nearly forty years after no-fault divorce laws were introduced in Australia, and while there were many books available on the stress that stepfamilies suffered, there was relatively little research or other information about their strengths. The adverse outcomes for children in stepfamilies was usually put down to a range of factors that had led to the change in family structure, including witnessing parental conflict or violence, having a parent with substance abuse issues or experiencing unstable housing.

However, Chandler Arnold from the US Center for Law and Social Policy (1998) says:

> Despite the fact that children in stepfamilies seem to be at greater risk of adjustment problems, most of these children are doing fine. According to clinical tests, between two thirds and three quarters of children in stepfamilies (and even more if the child is living in a well-established stepfamily) do not exhibit serious emotional or behavioural problems. In the long run, the response of most children to the challenges of life in a step-family seems to be characterized by resiliency and adaptability.

Why do some stepfamilies and blended families thrive when others founder? Studies show there are some key elements in building resilience for a new, complex family. A strong relationship between the couple at the heart of the new family is crucial to a stepfamily's robustness, considered the foundation for everything else, including the ability to handle stressors as they arrive. Strong emotional bonds between all members of the family are important, as are healthy communication patterns and systems.

Developing and using the right coping strategies at the right time and having family belief systems were also crucial. Support of the unit through the extended family is very beneficial, as, of course, is maintaining a respectful relationship with the non-resident parent. One way we developed our family belief systems was to copy from our local state school the 'Rights and Responsibilities' agreement idea—in which each class comes up with its own version of a social contract, that these are our rights as children but these are our responsibilities—and adapt it. That was an interesting process,

I assure you, but effective. So were the fridge magnets we put up, with quotes on them by Gandhi, Winston Churchill, Nelson Mandela, Martin Luther King, and Virginia Woolf.

Ross MacKay, from the New Zealand Ministry of Social Development, reviewed how children adjusted after divorce, and found that families who had flourished after the five-year milestone had had processes for solving challenges. Those processes, and not the number of challenges the family experienced, were the 'X factor' that helped them remain healthy and cohesive. Families who were thriving at the five-year mark had been flexible enough to recognise which processes didn't work and abandon them in favour of new ones, so as to discover over time what did work.

Chandler Arnold had another reassuring finding, that: 'Stepparents are not necessarily any less well-equipped to handle parenting situations than biological parents, rather stepfamilies are forced to confront problem areas biological families are able to avoid'. Stepfamilies need to tackle head on issues such as finding a compromise regarding each parent's child-rearing ideals, financial arrangements for child support, who plays which roles and what the expectations are, and stress management. There's no sweeping any of that stuff under the carpet! I have had to rethink my own operating model as a mum too. I have to consider the dynamics between the kids in a way I once didn't; as with most families, the rules and ways of teaching them change as they go through different stages, but I no longer hold fast to a particular model of parenting, and I'm always on the lookout for new developments in research, data and what works today.

For *Stepfamily Communication Strengths* (2003), Pennsylvania State University communication scholar Tamara Golish conducted in-depth interviews with ninety families and explains, 'In biological families, the roles and boundaries and management styles are enshrined in the stereotypes and stories we see every day.' Unconscious adherence to those stereotypes didn't help us in the beginning. Sometimes our confusion about who should respond to misbehaviour or decide on consequences was due to us basing it on the traditional roles of the mother and father; then we were advised that this would lead to disharmony and, potentially, rejection in the early years and rebellion in later ones. The message to me from all sources was that it is best the biological parent initially sets the rules in the early years. Now, after seven years, responsibility for administering discipline is more shared between Bill and me, and more accepted by the kids. He and the children learned to trust and love one another before he started to help me set and maintain boundaries with them, so the old adage about time healing was true.

For us, the right method has been to leave the disciplinarian role to me, with Bill as a support—which is certainly more practical, due to the demands of his work. Like many fathers, he is often working during the 'witching hour' and the hot-spot times around dinner. We also make sure the rules in our house apply equally to the three children, and abide by the Montessori principle that what's not okay at twenty years of age is not okay at two years of age either.

Mealtimes became central to us all connecting and building a stable routine. My neighbours and our wonderful babysitter (who came for the first weeks after Clementine's birth and has been a friend since) were hugely important fixtures in our collective landscape. My besties and their kids and our favourite neighbours would often be at the table with us. It was usually very noisy, with quite a bit of singing going on. The dishes were a mix of my childhood recipes, Nonna's soups, the babysitter's salads, and some new favourites the kids have asked for after eating them at their friends' places. Very Melbourne.

I found that as an immigrant to Victoria, forming some friendships with women who were also not from there originally was extraordinarily comforting. These women, with their older, thriving children, helped keep me together in the days, weeks and months after the big move and Clementine's birth; we have albums of shared memories now. They have been an immeasurable gift to me and our little family.

So, what helped us grow stronger in the early days were really the classic ingredients of any thriving family: warmth, affection and approval. Our family worked to build a shared history, told each other stories from the past, and looked through each other's photo albums, videos, and even childhood slides, to explain the missing pieces of time to each other.

When things were tough, though, we sought help from psychologists specialising in family counselling. It is important to find a practitioner who is not just an expert on families but on 'complex' families. Australia is blessed with brilliant and dedicated minds in this field; amongst others are Jan Nicholson; Matt Sanders; Michael Carr-Gregg; Steve Biddulph, on raising boys; and Melinda Tankard Reist, on respecting girls. As well as often visiting the *Stepfamilies Australia* website, I read about the work of the Family Action Centre in Newcastle, and that of Frank Oberklaid, from the Melbourne Royal Children's Hospital—who is justifiably known as the grandfather of paediatric public health.

I came across a study showing the stronger the skills of communication, negotiation and bonding the parenting couple had, the better they were at it (which is, as my kids would say, a 'no-brainer'). We took this list to our dinner table, and agreed the bonds were tight but the communication could do with some polish. Tamara Golish believes 'the more communicatively skilled a stepfamily is in identifying its strengths and weaknesses, the more likely it is that it can function effectively'. So, I upped the ante on family meetings, emails, letters left by the bed and messages on the bathroom mirror.

In the early years, I think I sent mixed messages to Bill about what he should and shouldn't do, and it plainly confused us both; sometimes I would think the children wanted him to be at some school or sport or music event when, in fact, it wasn't the case. Looking back, I realise I was trying to anticipate the kids' needs, instead of talking through exactly what their expectations were and how we might meet them. Had I known how important it was to sit down together, even at their tender ages, and role-play or talk through who does what, and what we could all expect, I would have been doing it every night!

Looking back, I think Bill and I would both agree with the dynamic sociological duo Marilyn Coleman and Lawrence Ganong, whose work on managing expectations in stepfamilies is the foundation of most new research. They found, time after time, that 'Unclear norms, expectations, boundaries, and relationships can be a source of significant conflict for many stepfamilies' (2001).

Whenever we stood fast to the idea of what a nuclear family would do, and how they would act in a situation, it wasn't helpful. If there were father–son or father–daughter days and we assumed the kids wouldn't want Bill to go, even though their dad couldn't be there, we were doing this based on stereotypes and on too strictly interpreting the names of the events. I think when, in the early days, I would go instead, it wasn't the right call. The children didn't say anything to us about it—more than half the kids at the school had fathers who couldn't go because of work—but I felt it was a missed opportunity for them, us and their classmates.

Garrett Pace (2015) from the Center for Research on Child Wellbeing at Princeton University agrees these kinds of issues can be disruptive. He found that clear communication, and unambiguous roles and expectations, is good for couples and for the kids! He says that what is needed is:

> Clear communication between spouses, which includes discussion of personal problems, ability to sit down and talk with a partner, and the opportunity to express oneself to their spouse. Our results show that the ability to clearly communicate and discuss problems with a spouse partially mediated the negative influence of step-parenting issues on satisfaction and stability in remarried couples.

He discovered that stepfamilies that were thriving were open with each other, spent time together, had clear rules and boundaries, solved problems together, and nurtured a positive image of the non-custodial parent.

Another report I found very useful early on was by Dr Jeremy Robertson from the Roy McKenzie Centre for the Study of Families in New Zealand. In looking at what made stepfamilies resilient, he interviewed forty-four of them and asked them about the four issues such families most commonly faced: who disciplined the kids and how; how they reached agreement on household rules and routines; how a respectful relationship with the non-resident parent was sustained; and how they managed to give enough time to the couple's relationship, especially if the parents had busy schedules. The families' answers demonstrated skill in facing the stressors and putting plans into place with flexibility and humour.

Routines have needed to be fairly flexible in a household like ours that sometimes resembles an airport lounge. Bill's responsibilities have to be redistributed when he's travelling, so I try to ensure the really crucial ones that often fall to men, like bin duty, aren't just his! As for agreement on the rules, they are constantly in negotiation now that we have teenagers, but for a few lovely years they ran like clockwork, with reward charts we've kept to show the kids in the years to come. Helping them become adept at managing their own routines has been important to their developing independence and self-esteem, but also a necessity given that they have three parents, two homes and lots of commitments.

In a, now famous, study done for US military personnel on deployment, RAND Corporation commissioned research by Lisa Meredith and others into promoting psychological resilience (2011), so as to identify the factors that servicemen and women require. The study initially focused on military families, but also looked at community aspects of resilience, such as a sense of belonging, cohesion, and a group's members' perceptions of their ability to work together.

The factors have since been adapted to many other realms, including the family and for building resilience in vulnerable children. Since encountering the study, I've employed these resilience factors as often as possible for both the kids and me. They include external ones, such as the way we utilise social supports; and internal ones: personal modes of operating, such as positive coping, positive affect, positive thinking, realism, behavioural control, physical fitness and altruism. Specifically, the factors as applied to a family, include emotional ties and bonding, incorporating common interests and activities; good communication, including exchanging thoughts on problem solving and relationships (which our family formalises with our discussion at lunches and dinners); support; and the perception that comfort is always available when needed, closeness, love, intimacy and attachment, nurturing, parenting skills and adaptability.

For those like me, who have a partner who is away for work for large amounts of time, military, political, fly-in fly-out workers and, increasingly, businesspeople and those who are sole parents, these factors are especially valuable family knowledge.

Dr Jeremy Robertson's study included families from Maori communities who had a strong support network and shared beliefs around religion, both of which were identified as helpful. My little family all have different views on coming to church with me, but we are united by our interest in such problems as inequality and poverty. This is fostered by the activities we do together and the community-focused ethos of the kids' schools. Exposing our children to community-based organisations that run outreach services, such as providing free meals, care of the elderly and disabled people, and having them visit kids undergoing challenges in their lives, has been a great way for us to help our children feel connected to something larger and more meaningful than just one family. Also, like families in the study, we have derived a lot of togetherness and enjoyment from doing these things together.

Practical things that helped us find our places in the new family order have included making sure we all have time together, as a whole unit and separately—for example, me with the older kids, and me with the little one; Bill one on one with each of them. We create space for these smaller groups to be together, but make sure we have defined times to get together to discuss rules and roles too.

We include the children in decision-making when appropriate, possibly even more than would be the case were we a nuclear family, as we are conscious of giving the children, who may feel powerless over their situation in a time of flux, the sense they have influence, and that their perspectives and wishes are taken into account. As well as helping build the resilience of our family, this sense that everyone is included equally strengthens the ties that bind us.

4

Don't listen to the haters

LOOKING BACK NOW, I see how resilient the children were during a period of immense change. It was a huge amount for them to deal with and they handled it with enormous grace.

I recently asked Gigi, 'What are the best things about us forming this stepfamily?', and she said, 'Clementine, Bill and Melbourne.' She was so clear about it that I was intensely reassured. Similarly, I asked Rupert the other night, 'Are you glad we did this; are there any regrets and, if so, what are they?', and he said, 'No, it's the right thing.' You can never be sure children are not just saying what they think you want to hear but I was heartened when they said those things to me.

Change always challenges us. And our family went through many of the events psychologists describe as among life's most stressful moments—divorce, moving house and cities, changing schools, parents changing their work status, change in the family formation—all colliding over about four months. Bill and I married in November, I moved in December, the baby arrived just before Christmas, and the children moved in January. And there had been all the lead-up to the wedding, and the media attention, which was another stressor for the kids.

I look back and think, 'How did we get through that?', but then I look at all the structures we quickly built around the new family unit and I know. We did it one day at a time. As well, I had an unshakeable faith in Bill's love for me. And one thing he did that was incredibly helpful in bonding with the kids, especially Rupert, was just to hang out. Read together, kick the soccer ball at the park, talk cards (even though Bill could *never* nail those Yu-Gi-Oh! cards; mind you, I didn't even try after my first attempt) and explore Melbourne.

Then the two of them got into road trips. These were a memory-making event like none other in my own childhood and something I remember with huge fondness. Still, thanks to those Chevy Chase *Vacation* movies, it was with some trepidation that I would wave the boys off.

Heaven knows what my parents were thinking when they packed up five kids, and all of our gear, and rolled out of the drive-way to another destination they felt featured 'important stuff' we should learn about, or just for a holiday. There was the Canberra trip to the Australian War Memorial and the High Court; to our friend's cattle property; to our cousins in New England; and count-less drives to beaches for family reunions, trips to relatives' farms, country towns, or to the mountains for a glimpse of snow. What you tend to recall from trips like these is all the fun and the sense of adventure—not the heat, the fights, the boiling-hot motel or the blue-lip-producing freezing pool, although those notorious incidents are good for some laughs now.

It must have been hideously stressful for my parents doing those long drives, but I never once heard them snap at one another, even when the car broke down during a Christmas heatwave. I remember tightly squeezed, sweaty, windows-down trips, with us elbowing each other, and all the while our parents calm and oblivious to the circus in the back. This is in striking contrast to my tolerance for even relatively short-distance car trips now; a few hours is enough to put me in a very unpleasant mood, so when we all have road trips together, Bill takes the wheel.

When we first started establishing our road-trip tradition as a new-look family, Bill was focused on getting to the destination and not stopping too often—other than to cope with the odd car-sickness-related-vomiting or wet-nappy incident. But, seven years on, now the children are older, we stop a *lot* and voluntarily take a whole day to get to our destination, rather than rushing there in a few hours. So, we have dismissed the notion of getting from A to B as fast as possible, and allow ourselves space for side trips, distractions and mistakes—much like what I would consider to be a healthy approach to remarriage. Even though I don't have my parents' patience for long-distance car travel, the advantages easily outnumber the disadvantages.

Another reason we choose to travel by car is the therapeutic benefits of spending time together in an enclosed space and sharing this experience. As the parenting experts tell us, the car is the perfect place to have awkward conversations, and to delve into kids' mind-bending questions such as 'Who is God?' or 'What's the future of our generation?'. I've read that not making eye contact during difficult conversations lowers the body's level of stress in response to them, so maybe having these kinds of chats in the car really is the answer. When Rupert was twelve, he and Bill set off on an epic 12-hour road trip. A thousand kilometres, four fast-food joints, six movies and a night in a motel later, they discovered they had covered a lot of conversational ground by looking straight ahead when travelling into emotional territory.

I have a pal who, four years ago, decided to have a child and raise him alone, and is also a great fan of the car heart-to-heart. Their conversation turns to all the things he talks about in child care, and anything else on his preschooler's mind. My friend, who is a neuro-scientist and the sole parent of a little boy, though with a very close circle of relatives and friends, makes a valuable point regarding talking to kids about their family situation; in her case, the choice not to parent with a partner: 'It strikes me as funny that the kids often don't associate it with something missing unless the other kids raise it. It's always good strategy to get out of the gates early and tell their friends' parents, so it's not raised first in the playground.'

The rhythm of my family's lives is anchored in new traditions and rituals, both everyday and celebratory. Like other stepfamilies, blended families, and all the other non-nuclear and traditional families in Australia, we are bound by the particular bookmarks of our family life.

Stereotypes about stepfamilies are rarely positive, and often potentially harmful to fragile new families if they are dragged up. Before I read the research on the stereotypes and stigmas imposed on non-nuclear families, I didn't realise how powerful these messages are, and how detrimental: the difficult kids trying to sabotage the new marriage; the 'wicked stepmother', the mean or neglectful stepfather—the malevolent spirits sent to menace unfortunate children and whose presence in their lives means they can never be the same again. According to well known Australian–New Zealand psychologists Jan Pryor and Bryan Rodgers, 'Historically, the stepfamily is portrayed negatively in fairy tales and in mythology, with stepmothers particularly maligned as "wicked".

Contemporary research findings perpetuate this view, with many studies emphasizing the risks to children in stepfamilies' (2001). US researchers Marilyn Coleman, Lawrence Ganong and Mark Fine tell us that 'too few studies identify factors and processes that facilitate the development of healthy couple functioning and stepfamily relationships' (2000). (Don't we know it.) Even life-long stepfamily advocates Emily and Dr John Visher noted that stepfamilies are often viewed through a nuclear-family lens, which can maintain unhealthy stepfamily myths, privilege the biological-parent role and stigmatise step-parent roles.

Again, the social mores, laws and expectations that have developed from the nuclear-family model have been useful, but with an increasing number of children living in other types of families, we need to find ways to make them, and their families, feel included. It's in all our interests to recognise, understand, encourage and support the wellbeing of all families, telling the stories of 'unusual' households without judgment. Well-adjusted, happy children are the well-adjusted and productive adults of tomorrow. The 'official' view of what is normal needs to catch up with reality.

As I continued to search out reference points for our family, and our vision of ourselves as one, I started looking for movies and TV shows that would help us focus on our strengths, and on what makes stepfamilies successful over time. I was looking for role models; my parents' marriage wasn't going to do the trick and nor was my godparents', which, as well as their parenting, I grew up admiring. Having role models helps people like athletes, artists, surgeons and entrepreneurs, so why not step-parents? Unfortunately, such role models in books and films are still very thin on the ground.

In her renowned book *The Remarried Family: Challenge and Promise*, which looked at the portrayal of stepfamilies, Esther Wald

(1981) showed depictions of step-parents in the fairytales of the Brothers Grimm, Hans Christian Andersen, and in all the other post-Renaissance children's tales, to be 'frightening and frightful', inspiring the idea that step-parents were not to be trusted and would not love their stepchildren properly. Our children's ideas of heroes and heroines are influenced from a young age by fairytales like those of Hansel and Gretel, Cinderella and Snow White. All of these endure, partly thanks to Disney, and infrequently paint a positive picture of stepfamilies. (Incidentally, Cinderella's story is so old, it harks back to ninth-century China.) Celebrity stepfamilies are easy to find, as so much paparazzi revenue is created from focusing on their stories—there are the families of Goldie Hawn and Kurt Russell, Tom Hanks and Rita Wilson, Daniel Craig and Rachel Weisz, Will Smith and Jada Pinkett-Smith, to name a few (and this is all without mentioning the Kardashians!). While most of those are regarded as highly functional family units, the glow around them hasn't extended to non-famous stepfamilies. To me, it is a bit of a mystery. Perhaps it's because a non-celebrity family's life isn't reported on?

It's not as if stepfamilies are some kind of modern anomaly; they were consistently common among historical elites: popes, kings and queens, biblical figures, were all involved in stepfamily situations. Royal families were very often stepfamilies; sometimes, many times over. Princes William and Harry have a stepmother; their mother, Diana, Princess of Wales, was a stepchild, as was Barack Obama. Television and movies have given us some notable stepfamilies: *The Brady Bunch, Blended, Step Brothers, The Parent Trap, Cinderella, Clueless, Stepmom, Garden State, Monkey Trouble* and *Modern Family* all frame their comedy and drama around the non-nuclear-family model.

The huge success of *Modern Family* gives reason for optimism that, at last, non-nuclear families, in all their messy glory (and all families have plenty of moments of messy glory, no matter what shape they take), are becoming mainstream and that the old stereotypes may be starting to lose their power. *Modern Family*'s success lies, I believe, in its ability to capture the humour and humanity of parenthood in all its guises and give parents in families of any variety permission to be imperfect—loving, safe and consistent but imperfect all the same.

Still, progress in this area is slow. Other than *Despicable Me*, I couldn't find one children's film with an uplifting story about a non-traditional family, even though we all loved Felonius Gru, a villain who became a sole dad, and then a hero for the love of his three little girls. On-screen families are still mostly Mum, Dad and their biological kids, even though this increasingly fails to represent the audience. As Esther Wald puts it, blended families 'live through an experience without society's understanding of what that experience is like'.

The still-common negative stereotypes about non-nuclear families affect how people in them feel about themselves, and can lead to pessimism about the potential of stepfamilies, and other non-nuclear families, to solve their problems and thrive. While living in the family I created with my first husband, I never questioned whether or not we could 'fix' things when they needed work. I find that now I'm in a stepfamily, there is a doubt that comes simply through perceived ideas about stepfamilies being less robust when faced with new and difficult situations.

This may be in part because the prevailing idea about remarriage, according to Andrew Cherlin's groundbreaking research (1978), is that it is an 'incomplete institution' that 'lacks clear social norms or guidelines for role performance or resolving problems'. Further, cultural understandings that the media and pop culture perpetuate—the modern folk tales—generally fall into one of two categories: either stigmatising stepfamilies, or creating unrealistic expectations, such as the myth of instant harmony and love (Ganong and Coleman, 1997).

Given that about 75 per cent of divorced adults remarry or cohabit with new partners, and given that remarriage or cohabitation sometimes occurs within months after beginning the new relationship, and many repartnered couples are simultaneously becoming part of a couple and negotiating step-parent–stepchild relationships, there is a large demographic of people living with perceptions, or assumptions, about their new situation that are either unduly negative or unrealistically optimistic. In other words, there is too much bad news and not enough realistic good news about stepfamilies.

I've felt deeply the intensity of the bias against and stereotyping of these 'other' family groups, and I've heard about it from mothers and fathers I have met and chatted with across the country. There is so much diversity among the stepfamilies I have encountered that they cannot be stereotyped; when I was young, I knew a girl whose stepfather was her biggest champion, and with whom she remained living after her mother's marriage to him ended when she was a young adult. Most of the step-parents I have spoken to in the past few years—and I have tried to talk to as many as I can— have seemed to be warm, generous parents, and deeply committed to their stepchildren, in so many ways.

Personally, I felt more self-conscious about our new non-conformity when in my home town than I have in Melbourne. Perhaps that was due to my connections in Brisbane being mostly people from 'traditional' families, or because many of my friends and contacts there knew me before my divorce, and took a little time adjusting to the change. I've noticed that even the kindest compliments I get from my original Queensland circle sometimes reflect the so-called 'deficit' model of thinking about divorced and remarried people—that they start their new relationship with a handicap. The comment from a dear friend that 'I never even think of you as a stepfamily, ever,' which was meant as a compliment, still implies 'I see you as somehow better than what I'd expected a stepfamily would be.' The commonly asked question 'How are the children coping?' is presumptuous, as is another comment I hear occasionally: 'Isn't it great how he's taken on the kids?'

Despite being surrounded by people in long-lasting marriages, I was fortunate during my formative years not to have received negative ideas about stepfamilies or other family formations that varied from the 'norm'. My parents were a bit ahead of their time, I suppose, as we were exposed to so many different types of lives through the community work and campaigning for children's rights they did. Over their eleven years in vice-regal roles, Mum and Dad got to know people from so many different backgrounds that they were very well informed about the diverse families in society. In the early 1980s, my mother ran the Australian Government's Women's Information Service in Queensland, and every day met with women in all kinds of situations to discuss with them what was going on in their lives, and I never heard a word of judgment, even though our own lives were pretty traditional. I never thought there was anything broken about non-nuclear families except when we heard about instances of family violence.

Early in the life of our stepfamily, my assumptions were tested only in so far as my idea that we could be just the same as a nuclear family. That was a learning curve. Thankfully, our family counselling sessions beforehand schooled me a little in what to expect: for example, that roles would still exist but who performed them might change. We put into practice advice about starting our own new traditions, rather than trying to mimic the way a nuclear family would necessarily do things, hence the road trips Bill and Rupert have to stay in touch with each other, find space in which to foster their relationship and build their database of common memories.

Another little ritual that works well for us is a technique we call the 'high-low', which is designed to survey, in a quick and not too probing way, how each of us is feeling. At the dinner table, we ask the kids to tell us about their experiences that day, and then validate their feelings, recognising there are vital lessons in both the good and the bad stuff they tell us. Because these exchanges are quick, they don't put anyone on the spot too much, but open the door for follow-up conversations and send the kids the signal that anything they feel is all right. Our other friends now do this with their kids at dinner too.

Another of our new traditions is all of us dressing up at Halloween, which was not a big thing in Brisbane but definitely is in Melbourne. Bill and I have been known to dress up with our local parents' group and surprise unsuspecting neighbours (which the kids thought was terribly funny when they were younger … I'm not so sure the older two do now they're teens!) We also have a swear jar, which is a great leveller, and the money from anyone in the family who drops a swearword goes to a charity we've selected. We have movie nights, where we take turns to choose or we vote for a movie, and we sit together watching it, with no one under pressure to talk; we can just be.

We use technology to stay in touch with each other, and with cousins on my side of the family (nine in Brisbane, three in Sydney); two Shorten nieces and nephews; and about a million of Bill's cousins, all in Melbourne. Technology has been a critical part of managing the transition to, and travel involved in, stepfamily life. FaceTime, Skype and Instagram have revolutionised our ability to stay intimately and regularly connected with family members who don't live near us. It gives the children some control over how they connect, and has led to some classic occasions, such as sharing on social media the loss of a tooth. We are also trialling a new Stepfamilies Australia mobile app to help us manage our calendars and keep the kids in touch with their dad's plans too.

Advice to put the health of the couple relationship high on the list of family priorities, and to let the children know this matters, was extremely useful. For the family to be cohesive, the parents need to be a solid unit. How important this is came home to me in a chat I had with a family friend of ours, a grandad in his seventies, who said that, in retrospect, he had not been prepared for stepfamily life. He told me he regretted not establishing with his children, who were then young adults, that his and his new wife's relationship was the foundation of their new family. 'If I had to do it over again, I'd make sure they knew I was on her side,' he said. 'And that she felt that too.' Also, he said it was a mistake simply to assume—as in old-school film and TV portrayals of stepfamilies—that everyone would just get along.

When we enter a new family unit with unreasonably high expectations, we put pressure on everyone: to form instant bonds of love, to play the traditional mother or father role and, often, to do it while courtship is still occurring. For me, lowering Bill's and the children's expectations of what I wanted from them was imperative. This was part of the advice we had received: to let the family develop over time, rather than try to force anyone into an uncomfortable position. I think had I explained this to the kids, too, it would have taken some pressure off them, but I thought they were too young to comprehend it. I also thought Bill and I assuming the traditional nuclear-family roles would give them more security, which was not the right call. I had to moderate the roles a little, and dial down my own fantasy that it would be easy to create boundaries through routine and strong discipline.

I found an excellent book about communicating with kids after a divorce, *Helping Your Kids Cope with Divorce the Sandcastles Way* (1999), by New York counsellor and rabbi M Gary Neuman. While the title might sound schmaltzy, it is a very specific and insightful book, and I wore the pages into tissue paper and dog-eared them like mad. What made it unique in my reading was that it actually role-played the conversations between parents and kids, and was so helpful I used it daily and even got a copy for the kids' dad. This book gave us the ability to express ourselves to each other at a time when the right words could be elusive, given all the emotion and confusion we were experiencing.

We learned from our Brisbane counsellor that trying to make a facsimile of a nuclear family (which is how stepfamilies were portrayed on TV and in movies for decades) does not guarantee the best possible relationships, and that the step-parent is better off not trying to assume the same operating model as the biological parent's. In other words, find a new role—that of a friend and supporter. This is often hard for stepmothers, who usually find themselves taking on the home-making, nurturing role, despite changes in gender roles. Stepmothers tend to bend over backwards compensating for the fact they are not the biological mother, and to assume the function of household go-to person, which can become unsatisfactory and unduly stressful. We need to support women not to do this to themselves!

Through my research, I discovered that the step-parent does better if they adopt a less active disciplinary role, and establish a more positive relationship with stepchildren than that of the traditional 'disciplinarian' and enforcer of rules, particularly in the formative stages. It seems that when the biological father assumes more responsibility for limit-setting behaviours, this is better for the stepmother. All the experts whose work I read concurred that when fathers and stepmothers agree on child-rearing issues, the stepmothers feel better about their marriages. This positive feeling can be, and often is, reflected in more positive relationships with stepchildren. None of this means the step-parent has to be overly permissive or ignore the tenets of good parenting generally; to put it in Hollywood parlance, it is like being the Best Supporting Actor or Actress.

5

Recognising the turning points

'Life is not meant to be easy but ... take courage, it can be delightful!' So said George Bernard Shaw in his play *Methuselah*, but Australians know the first part of this quote because our twenty-second prime minster, Malcolm Fraser, was unjustly mocked for saying, 'Life wasn't meant to be easy' in a speech. However, what didn't get reported was that he also said, 'but take heart, it can be wonderful!' I heard these optimistic words many times in my home when I was growing up and love their realism. When I was first married to Bill, I bumped into Malcolm Fraser's famously pretty and witty wife, Tamie, who was encouraging about my new baby and stepfamily, and very understanding about what it is like to have a husband working a long distance from home. I've met many women with a breadth of experience who have understood the reality of families and their changing forms, and many of whom have hailed from country towns and a life on the land.

My conversations with academics, sociologists and demographers, and my reading of the relevant research, confirmed my instinct that my family represents how much the face of 'the Australian family' is changing. While I was writing this book, even more new information came to light about just how fast and how widely what we consider 'the norm' is changing.

In October 2016, the Australian Institute of Family Studies released its sweeping report into the changing shape of our families, *Growing Up In Australia*, which found no less than 43 per cent of Australian children under thirteen have lived in what the AIFS has rebranded 'complex' families. This new, catch-all title is designed to encompass the many varieties of family that have joined the nuclear family in being common in our country: stepfamilies, single-parent families, families in which grandparents are raising the children, same-sex-parent families and families in which the parents have separated. In the study, spanning a decade, the AIFS found more than two in five children were living in complex families, with a sole parent, a non-biological parent, step or half-siblings, or grandparents.

The AIFS pointed out that while the term 'complex' families may imply these environments are unusual, 'in fact "complex" households are very much mainstream'. The most common forms of complex families are those in which children live with a single parent or a non-biological parent figure. Though the large percentage of children living in complex family arrangements may have come as a surprise to some, in reporting the new research *The Age* interviewed one 15-year-old girl who summed up perfectly how usual 'complex' has become. Ariel Reyes told the newspaper that for her the idea of living in a nuclear family is simply 'weird', and that having a mum, a dad and a stepmum was normal. 'I always thought it was normal, I never realised I was different,' she said.

Her parents, Tania Jovanovic and Gus Reyes, divorced when she was a baby but she and her brother, Tolly, see both parents: 'I see my dad every day, because they come over all the time. It's all normal, I guess,' she continued. She found being part of a complex family had no negatives, and that having an extra parental figure around meant more adults she could ask for help and do things with. Her blended family celebrates Christmases and birthdays together, and even takes an annual camping trip collectively.

The AIFS's landmark longitudinal study of Australian children followed 8000 children across Australia for more than a decade. It found rising divorce rates and less stable de facto relationships had caused the increase in the numbers of children being raised in 'double-family' living arrangements or living in a multiple-generation household. The AIFS's director, Anne Hollonds, said the new family arrangements had the potential to impact both positively and negatively on children. For some, the presence of other adults in the family may improve children's wellbeing by, for example, increasing financial resources, and the extra adult help can help bring stability to family routines. However, she cautioned that some children find it difficult to move back and forth between two households, while also adjusting to parents having new partners and to new half- or step-siblings: 'These more complex family dynamics bring with them changes in family routines, relationships and responsibilities that can be confronting for some children,' she said.

And, though I hope and believe all the hard work in putting down roots, painstakingly building relationships, tending new bonds and creating new communities for complex families such as ours helps them to endure, come what may, the report cautioned that 'complex households can be more unstable, with children facing challenges from living with a single parent, non-biological parents or changes to parents' relationships or living arrangements'. But, with this in mind, and our hearts as full of as much optimism about the future as any other family has, I think it is important to highlight what new and established complex families can do to counter the idea they are less likely to succeed or that they are second-best family environments.

Like all families, stepfamilies are often joyful—even if this is not necessarily how we are portrayed. Like other 'happy' families, we work on it. We address the different needs and expectations of each person, our histories and hang-ups, and keep a constant eye on everyone's ages and stages, and on managing the ambiguities that come with shifting roles. This intense concentration on building and maintaining the new, or complex, family can, in my experience and from what I've heard in my interviews with others in non-traditional family set-ups, usher in wonderful changes for children: they can feel more invested in, safer, and part of something bigger.

I wish I had known at the outset that there are well-documented stages a stepfamily such as ours goes through while establishing itself. So much is now known about how this process plays out that researchers have identified phases that are as predictable (but different from) the stages of family evolution that nuclear families experience.

Just as the sequential 'engaged, married, pregnant, baby' phases help couples starting traditional families know what to expect and how to prepare, there are recognised stages through which step-families move. The AIFS has prepared a truthful and informative paper about the phases of forming a stepfamily: fantasy, confusion, crazy time, stability, commitment. In the fantasy stage, the new family is yet to be realised and an idealised version of what it will be like is created; in the confusion stage, everyone is feeling their way and finding their feet, their role and the style of the new situation; in the crazy time, each person is in the throes of adjustment and the inevitable hiccups surface (just as there are hiccups in any family); and then comes the, gradual and increasing, stability phase and the feelings of security that accompany commitment. Each stage of that cycle unfolds organically, and must be worked through and fully experienced, not rushed.

You may be understandably keen to see everyone settled, and the sense of newness replaced by a bedded-down routine, but impatience won't serve you well. Putting pressure on yourself your partner, or children to move faster than is comfortable will not make relationships, or understanding and comfort, in the new framework grow more quickly.

Similarly, according to Patricia Papernow, who has been a specialist clinician in stepfamilies for four decades, as families form, they go through seven distinctive stages. This held true for our family.

Each of the seven stages is important, doesn't last and is a natural part of a stepfamily's development. Many stepfamilies also find themselves in different stages in different areas of their family's functioning. The better the family communicates while passing through to the next stage, the healthier its connections become.

The fantasy stage
This is where the couple at the centre of the family falls in love. In this honeymoon period, the adults fantasise about starting anew, or rescuing each other, and the children, from a sad past; perhaps even protecting their new partner from their new partner's previous partner. Children fantasise that the step-parent is temporary and that their biological parents will reunite.

Immersion
The blinders come off, and the family starts to face up to the reality that it is a permanent arrangement and requires work. The children

may be beginning to get to know the step-parent, but the step-parent is still the outsider to the parent–child unit.

Often the step-parent feels left out of the family unit, or even rejected by their stepchildren, leading to resentment and confusion. Some step-parents, particularly stepdads, may take a step back from family life, in an effort somehow to be shielded from further hurt—which their partner may, in turn, interpret as a lack of desire to be part of the family. Some step-parents may then start to feel trapped in a 'no win' situation. Struggling stepfamilies may get stuck here, continuing to strain toward their image of 'being like a family' and feeling they are failing. Once the adults accept the realities of their different family form they can begin moving to the next stage of family development.

Awareness

At this point, acceptance deepens that 'we are living in a really different kind of family'. Blame and shame begin to be replaced by curiosity and compassion. Papernow says:

> The feeling that 'something needs to change' characterizes Immersion, Awareness, and Mobilization. Struggling stepfamilies strain toward 'becoming normal' and get stuck in cycles of blame and shame. In the Awareness stage blame and shame lift, replaced by deeper acceptance. Like the difference between responding to a two-year-old temper tantrum with 'something's wrong here and it must be you, or me, or the child. We have to fix this,' and 'Oh! Our child is having a temper tantrum!' said with no shame or blame, but with curiosity and compassion about what might be happening with the child and what might be needed.

Although some step-parents start looking earlier or later, this is often the stage at which step-parents start to look for support and advice in the relevant literature, from other stepfamilies or from experts—seeking reassurance and acknowledging they need assistance in addressing the problems they have identified. Sadly, all too often, stepfamily couples cannot find specialist advice. Fortunately, Bill and I were able to find well-informed experts who were able to help. This was when I started my forensic examination of, for example, articles and websites.

Mobilisation

This can be a period of conflict and constant negotiation. Sensitive topics, such as former partners, financial arrangements and discipline begin to be addressed if the family is to really move forward. More often than not, it is the step-parent who brings attention to the changes needed and shares their problems. In this stage, children who have been initially cooperative may begin to express their discomfort and unhappiness over all the changes in their lives. Struggling stepfamily couples get stuck here, fighting and blaming each other. Successful stepfamily couples, on the other hand, find constructive, caring ways to bring up differences. Over time, and as the prime relationship gains strength, the parents and step-parents begin to confide in each other about their experience of stepfamily life and what should be addressed. As understanding deepens, parents can begin helping step-parents feel less the outsider by providing empathy and understanding. Likewise, step-parents can begin offering more compassion for the parent's stuck 'insider' position.

Action

Working together during this stage is key to resolving the problems any stepfamily is likely to have. In this stage, the adults begin making decisions as a team, even if the parent is the one who implements disciplinary moves. This can take time, because good resolutions require understanding the feelings and needs on all sides, including some of the unpleasant feelings that have been experienced. As well, classic gender expectations may be disturbed. In my family, this was the turning point in becoming a more integrated, happier unit.

Contact and resolution

These are the final stages of accepting that the family has its own way of solving problems, its own roles, and rituals that connect and integrate it. Now the members feel more secure in their relationships with each other, more confident as a group and more resilient. Because stepfamilies bring together at least two very different already-established cultures, many differences may remain. But, as Dr Papernow says, the family has a solid sense of 'we-ness'.

Let's face it—no family is plain sailing all the time; it's important for step-parents to know its okay to pull back if things are not progressing as they would like. Some may never achieve closeness with their stepchild, and while this can be upsetting, it's important for them to accept this, value what is there and be open to letting what isn't there go.

Although these stages may appear distinct, they will usually merge into one another without seeming defined or perhaps even without the family being aware of the changes. Sometimes they operate more like 'stations' that get visited in a distinctly non-linear order on the way to Contact and Resolution. It is only with the benefit of hindsight that you see subtle shifts in relationships. Some families will take longer than others to move through the stages, and, although there is no hard and fast rule, it's typical for even very successful stepfamilies to take several years to reach the final phase. Just try to work out where you are in the cycle with the important issues in your stepfamily, and think about what you need to change within the family to enable it to evolve.

Having that horizon of five years somewhere in the back of my mind helped me. Sure enough, as the calendar flipped over five years on, I felt we were safely in the 'resolution and acceptance' stage, though sometimes we slipped back to needing to revisit 'working together'. We are now in our eighth year and cherishing family life together.

One thing Bill noted, as I did in my wide reading about the formation of stepfamilies, is that while 'advice' about how step-mothers could integrate into families in which their new partner had children but they had not yet had a child together was plentiful on social media and in personal accounts, there was a dearth of 'accessible' material relating to, or for, stepdads. Almost all of the research is about stepfather families but it's not readily available to these families or to clinicians. Where there was anything concerning stepfathers, it was always in a chapter at the end, in what felt like an afterthought. The one piece of consistent informa-tion–slash–advice on stepfathering that we could find was simply to remember that, while you are not the children's father, you can do 'dad-like things' in their world.

Bill, like most stepfathers, was anxious to be a decent parent, and had not had kids in his first marriage. Some stepfathers who did have children in their earlier partnerships have suggested they wanted to make up for the first time around, reflecting that they were motivated to be closer to the children from subsequent rela-tionships than they had been to their first set of kids. Sometimes, unfortunately, these expectations are in conflict with children's need to keep some distance. Too, some note their new partner expects them to play a more equal parenting role. The research is clear about this. Step-parents need to begin by what Papernow calls 'connection not correction'. Parents need to retain the disciplinary role until or unless step-parents have established a trusting caring relationship with their stepchildren. This is more likely and may happen more quickly with children under eight. In many healthy stepfamilies, step-parents do not have a disciplinary role.

I had expectations of Bill—that we would share the workload, domestic, economic and parenting, but I didn't have any particular model of parenting in mind for him to follow. I saw him as a father figure with P-plates on at first, and referred to him having inherited 'instant noodles': two fully formed kids.

I asked Bill what stuck with him about people's responses to his new status as a stepdad; what was helpful and unhelpful in the early days; and what he tried and dropped along the way to finding a natural sense of stepfatherhood. On the upside, he noted that while some people surprised him by not coping with his status as a stepdad, lots of people were 'the exact opposite, not judgmental at all—supportive and encouraging'.

He learned to relax about his parenting skills (or lack thereof, according to him). He observed that 'people are not always judging you; they are often too busy with their own lives', and that, while some could be thoughtless with the language they used about family, many people's attitudes confirmed the AIFS's subsequent finding that most understand the new normal to include many varieties of family groupings. Unlike me, he did not find a noticeable stigma against stepfamilies.

I asked Bill what he regarded as the most useful advice he had received during our family counselling: which had proven practical in day-to-day stepfamily life. This included don't be impatient; do make time for the family; don't miss a minute if you can possibly avoid it—they grow up quickly—and do back your wife in her dealings with the children. (This guidance is supported by the research—the most effective step-parents begin not by stepping in and taking over, but by backing up their partners.) He also said the advice to ask other dads what to do and to share experiences was very helpful, and he puts this into practice on regular runs with a close friend who is a great dad. Other good advice was to prioritise family holidays, establish rituals and 'do what kids want to do (together), as opposed to what you want to do'. The advice not to argue very much in front of the kids was beneficial (and also supported fully by the research—children with divorced low-conflict parents are doing significantly better than children of never-divorced high-conflict parents), as were basic hints, such as when you're at home, be at home, and not on your phone; don't push conversations with the children, listen to them; and don't push them to bond quickly, but share their interests and build an affinity first.

It has been a delight to watch the relationships between Rupert and Bill, and Georgette and Bill, develop. Rupert enjoys the attention Bill gives him, taking him to Rupert's activities and to Bill's own engagements—through this, Rupert learned a number of Anzac Day songs, and picked up some skills in debating long before he was old enough to join the school debating team.

I remember when I started to realise Bill and Rupert had really connected with each other, and it was through small moments I witnessed but wasn't necessarily a part of, because it was something they were sharing as man and boy within their relationship. Bill has lots of 'credos' for life, and one of them is the Wesleyan one 'Do all the good you can, in all the ways you can, for all of those you can, as long as ever you can.' A couple of years ago, Bill was talking with Rupert and mentioned a Jesuit quote he'd learned at school, about how you become a man by doing things for other people. Rupert came back with 'Yeah, I know; and do all the good you can, in all the ways you can, for all of those you can,' gently teasing him that he already knew this and it had really sunk in.

Listening in on, or catching bits of, conversations like these that I wasn't actually part of was a great indicator that Bill and Rupert had really bonded. They were just shooting the breeze as mates— they have a similar sense of humour and their jokes are getting more alike; they share a funny bone. At times I've just walked past and taken the temperature of what's going on with them, and Rupert and Bill have been in hysterics. I've just looked at them laughing—probably about something highly inappropriate, maybe lines from *Monty Python's Life of Brian*, which they've watched together—and realised they have their own comedy language now. It's an intimacy I don't share, because I haven't seen the same movies they have, or shared the same jokes about things Bill has shown Rupert, or Rupert has shown him. I feel a bit on the outer but know they have a close relationship quite independently of me. And that feels extremely healthy.

Again, that feeling of being a little outside the original core group can be something step-parents struggle with. But what's really important for them, I think, is to reach for their partners for extra hugs and caring, not fight it. Not being part of the original group can sometimes be painful, even in well-established happy stepfamilies. Parents can help by continuing to provide full empathy for step-parents' outsider status. Papernow advises: 'What step-parents most need first is full acknowledgement and empathy for the reality and the feelings that go along with it. That compassion is comforting and regulating. Then they can sometimes hear what important roles they play.' The fact that another group existed before you came along needs acknowledgment, especially for kids who have been with one parent for quite a while after a divorce. You need to acknowledge that they have a special bond. Still, it can sometimes be hard to not feel as 'important' to that original group. Your partner's care and compassion will help a lot, as will yours for the fact that they are sometimes torn between your needs and those of their children.

While we're on the subject of what enriches the stepfamily unit, it's worth sharing a 'family strengths inventory' that researchers John DeFrain from the University of Nebraska-Lincoln and Nick Stinnett from the University of Alabama identified when they interviewed 17 000 people in twenty-seven countries about common threads in strong families. Families can use the *Creating a Strong Family: American Family Strengths Inventory* to help them identify, discuss and record the qualities that make them strong. The inventory asks families to take stock of the way they are as a family; discuss the strengths they identify; celebrate those strengths; identify strengths that could be improved and design a plan to build on them. Because the inventory is strengths-based, it will not tell a family what they are doing right or wrong but will help them to discover their strengths and potential for growth. I've been taking our family through the questionnaire, although it's taking forever to complete it between homework, sports, music practice and Netflix.

It was through reading about Stinnett's finding that families who thrive share six qualities that I found a lovely book, right up my constantly cooking alley, called *The Hour that Matters Most: The Surprising Power of the Family Meal* (Parrott, Parrott, Allen and Kuna, 2011). It's an inspiring look at the value of heading back to the dinner table together in this time-poor, fast-food world of ours, and so much of what they write about sounds like my house at times. The authors used Stinnett's research in suggesting the following 'secrets' of creating the safest place on earth. I have put them on a poster that I've subtly placed in a few spots at home (I'd put them in the car and the bathroom but the kids would kill me if their friends saw them; the quotes on the fridge are bad enough apparently!)

We share Commitment: each of us are dedicated to promoting one another's welfare and happiness.

We show Appreciation and affection: each one of us in this strong family are thankful for each other. We prize our relationships with each other.

We strive for Positive communication: we spend a lot of time talking freely with one another, just hanging out, to be understood and to understand.

We spend Time together: our family spends a lot of time with one another—even if we squabble over the TV—creating memories and building bonds.

We look after our Spiritual well-being: strong families, like ours, have a sense of greater good that gives us a joint purpose.

We have learned the Ability to Cope with stress and crisis: in this strong family we are not fragmented by tension and trouble. We use those experiences to learn and grow together.

And other researchers, Kelley and Sequeira (1997), have found that strong families exhibit these kinds of common elements: they are open; manage conflict; spend time together; create a supportive environment; are spiritual and feel a sense of unity. Spirituality can simply mean having a sense of something other than ourselves being important.

In fact, researchers have found that struggling stepfamilies face the same challenges that successful stepfamilies do. Successful stepfamilies practise many of these behaviours (Golish; Papernow, 2013). While looking for practical help on what to do, we found other words of advice that were very valuable in the developmental stages. I'd like to meet Dr Joan D Atwood, who is the director of

the graduate programs in marriage and family therapy and director of the Marriage and Family Clinic at Hofstra University. She
says that working on being a couple within the family group, even
while concentrating on making everyone feel part of one unit, is
vital: 'The marriage is the bonding unit that caused the stepfamily
to come into being. It requires nurturing if the stepfamily is to
continue in a healthy manner.' However, nurturing the marriage is
not *the* central task. In stepfamilies, very close couple relationships
are linked to poorer wellbeing in children, because as Papernow
explains in her book, children may not have enough access to
parent–child secure attachment. She says, 'carve out one-to-one
time for both the couple and parent–child relationship and for
step-parent–stepchild relationships'.

Atwood defines 'Ten necessary tasks in the achievement of
stepfamily integration'. I had the list of tasks on my fridge for some
time and would recommend others do the same!

One: Resolution of fantasised expectations

At the time of remarrying, a couple may have rosy expectations,
believing that the children will welcome the wonderful new person
who is entering their lives. From the children's point of view,
however, the picture may look very different. Many children of
divorced parents not only want their biological parents to reunite,
they don't wish to have the relationship they have with their custodial parent interfered with. The presence of another person in
a parent's life threatens both these wishes. For the adults, a new
relationship is a gift. For children it is a loss. Adults in love are very
engaged with each other. Parents often turn away from full attention on their children. Consequently, although the adults are eager
to move forward, children are often struggling with significant
losses, caught in loyalty binds with the other parent. Children often

need significantly more time than adults wish they did for adjustment to a stepfamily. Encouraging them to express their feelings and finding your compassion and empathy facilitate this. Former partners can be instrumental in this if they're willing to help the children adjust.

Two: Resolving mourning and loss issues

The process of divorce and the transition to remarriage create an almost universal feeling of loss and grief in both parents and children, and incomplete mourning can interfere with creating a successful new stepfamily. One way that mourning may be interrupted in the single-parent family is if either parent uses the children to get comfort and support, as the children haven't been permitted to experience their pain, which remains unattended to, because they're busy caring for their parent. Remarriage may rekindle these suppressed feelings for children, as they may fear losing their relationship with the custodial parent because of it. They may then behave angrily, which often leads to further loss.

After a remarriage, the children must share their parent with another adult, and perhaps with other children. They often inadvertently lose a significant amount of parental attention and wonder how often they'll see their biological parent. They may be deeply worried whether there'll be a place for them in the new household. Teenagers may be asked to give up their role of being an adult's companion and become a child again. Again Papernow warns that adults and kids experience stepfamilies very differently. 'One of the most important ways to support children in stepfamilies is to help adults be able to tell the story from the child's point of view,' she says.

There are also less obvious losses: the dream, even for the spouse who initiated divorce, of what the former marriage was going to be; or the expectations of what marriage would be like for some-one who has never been married and is marrying someone with children. Letting go of these fantasies can be so difficult that many people experience anger and sorrow before accepting reality.

So, when a divorce occurs, even if the marriage has been unhappy, the parents experience the loss of a dream. At the time of remarriage, the parents and, particularly, the children may still be grieving their respective losses. In addition, the children experi-ence a second loss when their custodial parent remarries. Again, the new relationship is a wonderful gift and a gain for the parent. It is often experienced as a yet another loss and way too much change for children. Empathic compassionate adult presence is what helps kids make this transition. The more upset, the more compassion they need, but the harder, all too often, it is for adults to get where kids are, Papernow tells us in her book *Surviving and Thriving in Stepfamilies*.

As a result of all of this, new step-parents face children dealing with loss, anger, guilt, rejection and despair. Struggling stepchildren need their parents, not their step-parents. Furthermore, some may need considerable distance from their step-parents. This can be very stressful for step-parents who have gone into a marriage believing their stepchildren will immediately love and appreciate them. They feel confused and disappointed when their stepchildren withdraw from them.

Three: Dealing with divided loyalties

Children often have divided loyalties towards their custodial parents and their step-parents. A child may view the step-parent as an intruder and cling to the custodial parent. As during a divorce, the child and the custodial parent are both experiencing a loss, they often form an exceptionally close relationship. When a remarriage occurs, the custodial parent or the children may have difficulty letting go of this. In addition, because it's difficult for the new partners to have time alone together, the step-parent may feel jealous of the attention the children receive. Thus, the step-parent has both a spouse and stepchildren with divided loyalties, often making the step-parent feel resentful and disappointed.

One way of handling such crises is to provide ample time and opportunity for these concerns to be expressed. Each family member must be able to talk about their feelings and contribute to finding effective solutions.

Four: Resolving issues with former partners

Studies have found that both spouses in a stepfamily are likely to experience stress due to three major problems: custody and visitation difficulties; the former partner's telephone calls, broken promises or late arrivals upsetting the children; and competition between the current and former spouse. In addition, the step-parent can feel jealousy if their partner has emotional baggage from their first marriage, stirring up anger and rivalry. This kind of unresolved emotional baggage is often as follows. That although spouses hope the remarriage will give them a new lease on life, they fear it won't last, because their last one didn't, and they fear repeating past mistakes. These fears can then become a self-fulfilling prophecy.

Finding a solution is often beyond the resources of the new family, so therapy can be the best solution. These issues are so emotionally charged, an objective viewpoint can be needed so as to resolve them effectively.

Five: Reducing role confusion

The step-parent's role becomes a measure of the stepfamily's development. The degree to which all its members have a meaningful role determines how well established the family and its rules will be in the eyes of the family members, other relatives and outsiders.

Perhaps the greatest source of stress in step-parenting is that the step-parent role is not clearly defined. The step-parent is a newcomer—often, the intruder or interloper—in an established family system. Initially, because the step-parent is an intruder, there may be an attempt, either overtly or covertly, to expel them. This upheaval may result from the children not knowing what to expect from the step-parent.

It is difficult to prepare to be a step-parent. There is no legally sanctioned role: the step-parent–stepchild relationship confers no rights and imposes no obligations. Circumstances can then reinforce the impression of the step-parent being a non-parent. However, the step-parent's role develops over time through shared experiences and their involvement with the family.

Six: Deciding on the role of discipline

Remarriage involving children brings with it instant parenthood, which is a major source of stress for the step-parent. A major problem step-parents have as they try to share the parental role is disciplining the children. Doing so effectively is key to the step-parent's integration into the family.

There are many issues around discipline that stepfamilies face. The adults may have different methods of discipline. The custodial parent may find it difficult to share the role of disciplinarian with the step-parent. The custodial parent may believe the step-parent is picking on their child; custodial parents often feel defensive, and may feel inadequate, when step-parents criticise their children. The child may refuse to obey the step-parent. If there were no children in the step-parent's earlier marriage, there is hence no prior parenting experience, and the custodial parent may have shown a lack of discipline during the period in which they were a single parent that spills over into the new situation. Often the step-parent remains an outsider when it comes to discipline, while the custodial parent functions as the sole authority figure. As a result, discipline-related matters are often left unresolved and the lines of authority remain unclear.

Seven: Something old and something new —the development of new traditions

When stepfamilies form, existing daily and personal activities are thrown into disarray. Things will never be the same again, and nor should they be. One immediate obstacle to becoming an integrated stepfamily is the numerous adjustments required, including new ways of doing things and, especially, changes in values.

Decisions need to be made about new roles, rules and traditions for the new household. In addition, meaningful traditions from any family member's past need to be maintained whenever possible. This demonstrates respect for individual members' preferred way of doing things, and demonstrates to the children that there is neither a right nor a wrong way of doing things. It should be emphasised that everyone's input is required to creatively develop effective solutions; this needs to be an ongoing process. In this way, important old traditions are maintained and new traditions develop.

Eight: Forming new interpersonal relationships

In a nuclear family, the couple has the chance to solidify their relationship before children arrive. This is not the case in a stepfamily, in which the new couple may be attempting to have a honeymoon in the middle of a crowd. Also, parent–child relationships have been of longer duration than the new couple's relationship. Frequently, children are dropped on the doorstep of a couple who hadn't planned to include them in their new household.

Everyone may feel uneasy and trapped. The biological parent may feel guilty about the unhappiness on all sides, and push for quick step-parent–stepchild relationships, increasing the tension. The guilt, anger and frustration may often be followed by feelings of rejection and alienation. If the dissension interferes with the marital relationship, this can be particularly devastating for the stepfamily unit.

Nine: Strengthening the marriage

The healthy development of a remarriage often suffers with the premature presence of children, as the demands of child-rearing may distract from, if not interfere with, it. Other family duties often short-circuit the couple finding time for each other, and many conflicting forces can weaken their relationship. For example, they may feel guilty about forming a new adult–adult relationship because it seems a betrayal of their parent–child relationships; there may be divisive behaviour on the part of the children, who may still retain the fantasy of their biological parents getting back together; there may be non-acceptance of the new partner and children by step-grandparents, or other close relatives; and there may be neglect of stepfamilies' needs by many institutions, such as schools, churches and the law. There may also be fear of repeating past mistakes; there may be inequality issues, such as unequal finances; there may be extended-family ties to the former partner, which can cause conflict.

These internal and external stresses for remarried couples require they make time to nourish their relationship, remembering that preserving a commitment to one another will stabilise the new household. Such a commitment is also a model for the children when they establish their own adult relationships.

The couple must set aside time to spend alone, both weekly and daily. Opening the lines of communication, keeping each other informed and involved in the daily activities of the household, is crucial. The children find marital emphasis comforting because they begin to see it as strong and united. They then can trust that it also will be strong and united for them. Such role modelling will aid the children in eventually separating from the family and establishing their own healthy adult relationships.

Ten: Household management

Another complex issue the newly formed stepfamily faces is how to financially and logistically manage the household's affairs. For example, Johnny has soccer practice; Anne-Marie has a dance recital; Paul has a dentist's appointment, and Mum has to do the grocery shopping. How is all this done between 4 p.m. and 6 p.m.?

Weekly meetings can be an effective way of managing these concerns. Goals can be identified and prioritised, and the means for achieving them be explored. This process needs to be done regularly so that personal feelings and thoughts can be aired. Each member of the stepfamily needs to accept that parents can't be all things to all children at all times, and family meetings provide the opportunity for members to express their feelings about what can't be.

So there seem to be three phases in achieving stepfamily integration. First, the family must establish a common history by sharing memories of the past. This requires coming to terms with the past in the context of the present, which is the second phase. These processes then trigger the activation of the family members' own inner resources. As issues that have been avoided are addressed, any feelings of being trapped by each other yield to a sense of possibility.

Obviously, the wellbeing of the children comes first but the path to the above phases starts with the importance of the parents' coupledom. Perhaps it was how things were in earlier times, when the period between betrothal and pregnancy was usually much shorter, but now it's an unusual experience to be simultaneously courting and parenting when you're first living together. Still, the dynamic of bonding with your mate while establishing your family means that time and energy need to be invested in your relationship, as this is the foundation for your stepfamily.

Bill's and my situation was particularly complex, in that having just married, we had a newborn, as well as two young children to settle in. So much in a short time and, like speed-dating and packet cakes, I wouldn't recommend it. Our honeymoon was a babymoon and Bill was, of course, an instant parent of three. While in nuclear families the couple usually has time to establish their relationship before the children come along, in other families it may all happen at once, and the fundamental building block on which everything else sits is the couple's relationship. Again, it must be nourished through spending time together; making time to talk daily; and, in our case, family meetings.

Sometimes kids feel jealous of the time their parent and step-parent are sharing and that is not devoted to them but, again, over time they will find it reassuring, both as proof of commitment to them, and as a model for their relationships when they establish their own families (though I've told my children they're not moving out of home until they're thirty-five!). The kids are so used to Bill and I having time as a couple, they just say, 'Ohhh, parent time … rigggght', except for Clementine, who stands between us when we embrace. I don't remember ever worrying about the strength of my own parents' marriage, and the fact I was able to take it for granted is something, all these years later, I'd like to thank them for.

La Trobe University is one of a few Australian institutions that focuses on the wellbeing of families and Professor Jan Nicholson is the first academic to head a comprehensive program on the transition to parenthood in contemporary society. Further backing up the points I've been making in this chapter, Nicholson says: 'The couple relationship in a stepfamily is critical. The family is only together because of this relationship. This is not to say that it is "more important" than parent–child or step-parent–child relationships. Rather, that it is the magnet that brought the family together, and over time it needs to be nurtured and protected.' She also told me: 'Starting early, and with a preventive focus, is important. We need to normalise seeking information and supports, so that people in any type of family, but especially stepfamilies, are empowered to obtain the information and resources that will help them to build a positive future together and handle the inevitable cascade of challenges that growing up as family brings.'

Bill and I have spent quite a lot of time learning together how to keep communication constant and open in such a busy household. We talk at the end of every day, no matter where we are, have weekly alone time, and even try to model resolving arguments in front of the kids sometimes. We let them know it's important and desirable for Bill and me to be together, and they feel comfort in this.

Being a couple doesn't just mean spending time alone and having date nights, though—it means showing a united front; the sense the two of you are in lockstep with each other. The children need to know you share parental authority. This helps prevent confusion, and heads off the risk of the kids developing alliances or playing the residential parent off against the parent they're not living with. It can reduce conflict, and ensures the step-parent doesn't feel like the permanent outsider.

Research has consistently found that, compared with first-marriage families, stepfamilies have been described as more stressful, more conflict ridden and less cohesive. Numerous studies have found children in stepfamilies have more frequent behavioural problems and turbulent relationships, distance themselves more from parents and have lower self-esteem than children of first-marriage families. One notable study found less positive couple communication and biological parent–child communication in stepfamilies than in first-marriage families.

Research that focused on the types of conflict in stepfamilies (Coleman et al, 2001), and the strategies used to resolve them, found it came from underlying issues of control and the negotiation of boundaries. Healthy resolution of conflict was inhibited when conflicts were hidden or left unresolved. Nevertheless, conflict was often a catalyst for improving stepfamily relationships, particularly when family members were able to compromise and communicate openly.

So how does our family communicate healthily and effectively, to solve conflict and knit together? We have employed a broad range of, sometimes unorthodox, tools to establish open talking every day. Over the years, dinner table and kitchen talk has centred around what's happened, and what's happening, in our daily lives. We use conversation-starting techniques, such as saying that whoever holds the serving spoon has the floor, and we play charades. I've given the kids journals over the years, and we've used them to write our thoughts to each other—just me and them. It was an avenue for them to share their concerns and for me to write mushy stuff without them getting embarrassed.

We can be a fairly rowdy group, and the children have collected a range of very funny anecdotes from life at our table, like the time Clementine, not yet two years old, looked up from her highchair and said her first sentence. Commenting on something the older children were discussing, she exclaimed, 'Well, that's random!' We've found bedtime is the best time for sharing difficult information, and when Bill and I are both home, we split up and spend time in each of the children's rooms as they are getting ready to sleep.

Over time, we have tried different methods to keep communication channels well and truly open. Trial and error has been very helpful and, as I talked about earlier, talking in the car is a winner for us. We all walk the dogs together by the Maribyrnong River, and during these walks Bill and I sometimes raise subjects such as how all change is stressful but that the stresses can be overcome, and then illustrate this with examples from our lives.

We try to encourage intimacy between each of us by being as patient as we can (which isn't always very) and, again, making regular time to listen to the kids. We keep an eye on their behaviour for anything that could signal they are having a rough patch: such as changes in sleeping patterns, losing interest in something they usually like, or being quieter than usual. We try to make the children feel they can talk about their expectations, including as regards respect and privacy, and about how they'd like to raise problems or sort out disagreements.

And we tell old stories. During my childhood, we put great store in rehashing stories and memories, looking at old photos and slideshows to see our parents and their families as children, and it was always great fun. My sister has a mega-memory and uses it to great effect at family gatherings, offering up hilarious accounts of one or another of us doing something out of the box. She is our memory keeper.

Your life before they came along is one of the things kids become more curious about as they get older; they like hearing about their parents' youth and, of course, hang out for any story about a parent's naughty behaviour. I carry on the tradition of keeping family memories front and centre by creating albums, including a digital one that I update regularly after family holidays. At the end of every year, I give each child a 'book' of their past year, which charts their activities, big challenges, small accomplishments, songs they've heard, books they've read and other memory minutiae.

Revisiting the past is also helpful because building a stepfamily unit is a little like time travel for some members. For Bill, it was as though he were fast-forwarded to the primary-school years, without the benefit of knowing Rupert and Gigi's kindy years and toddler times. Similarly, the kids were suddenly trying to get to know a lot about Bill in order to make a connection with him that made them feel secure. To help fill in the blanks in the lives of the new partner and the children they have not known from babyhood, you need, in a sense, to fast-track the links and knowledge.

Our 'scaffolding', as I call it, went up fast: the creation of rituals and new traditions was very grounding, as was setting up new systems and rules, roles and routines. Even so, we needed to be aware that one set of strategies will work one year but not so well the next. And that one set of strategies will work for one stepfamily and not for another. Family life, in whatever type of family you are living in, never stands still, and requires flexibility, creativity and adaptability to change. These qualities can help build resilience in all of you.

We have had regular family chats on the couch, where we've negotiated jobs, meal planning, weekend activities, work-travel planning and who will babysit, and our communication techniques have evolved, even in just the last couple of years. We have a family diary that used to detail everything the kids did in a day; now it records the older ones' appointments, our schedules and commitments, and Clementine's milestones, activities and eating habits. We have a whiteboard, the diary, texting, emailing and a joint iCalendar. Bill's weekly program is on the hall table, so the kids always have a sense of where he is. Things change frequently and weekly arrangements for the adults are fluid. This is sometimes tough for planning, so 'flagging', letting everyone know what might be subject to change—like flights—is a constant challenge.

But even with all of this work around communication that we are doing separately and together, communicating well under pressure at home is the skill I would most like to acquire. When one child has gastro, and one is due to meet a bus to go to camp, and another is suffering exam stress, and Bill is in a plane, and the dog has peed on the furniture, and I've slept badly for three nights—that's when I'm thinking, 'This wasn't in the brochure.' Even the trendy technique of mindfulness doesn't help, as at moments like these I don't actually *want* to be in the moment. Breathing techniques for relaxation, which you can usually learn at a yoga class or read about on the internet, do help.

I'm a professional communicator—I have formal qualifications and twenty years' experience advising on and managing communications in organisations. You'd think, as a result, communicating in a family setting would come naturally, but it often doesn't. Applying the right knowledge in the right place and at the right time is what parenting and internal family communication is about, but communication skills are hard won. Though I've read hundreds of articles by experts and other texts, including case studies, I've definitely not nailed it. So, go easy on yourself when your best-laid communication plans go awry.

The more skilled we are at understanding ourselves, our strengths and vulnerabilities, the better we interact as a group. All big transitions in a business, or any other organisation involving human beings, rely on good, clear understanding and communication—healthy families do too.

6

Five years on

IN THE SUMMER of 2014, Bill and I had been married for five years. For a traditional wedding anniversary, we would have been giving one another daisies and wooden gifts; we didn't (my attitude to the daisies-and-wooden-gifts idea was a bit 'Hmmm') but it felt like a milestone regardless. It had been sixty months, 260 weeks, 1825 days, of living together under one roof. (Well, two roofs, really, with Bill's lodgings in Canberra taken into consideration; or even three, if you count the kids' second home in Brisbane.)

The five-year mark was a turning point for us all. The children, who were all there, helped us celebrate our anniversary. Clementine started prep, which was also the first time Bill experienced the first day of school for one of his children; we found photos and videos of the older two starting school to connect him with the experiences he'd missed. Rupert and I walked Clementine to school, with the friends she calls aunties and our neighbours waving her off.

I was very fortunate that before Clementine started prep I could take time out of the workforce while Bill settled into his job as a minister in the federal parliament. I was able to concentrate on helping the children to put down roots, and devote some time to developing interests (such as singing jazz, writing, swimming and cooking) that I had put on the back-burner while having a big corporate workload during the older two kids' early childhoods. Plus, it was almost logistically impossible, with Bill's workload and travel, for me to be working outside the home.

Mothering has always been one of my interests; supporting all new mothers pays such dividends to our society. I was grateful to experience being a stay-at-home mum for the first time, and going back to work after having my third child was just like any other mother's experience.

I remember how the mothers' group in Brisbane I was in when I had baby number two was so motivated to support one another and other mums we knew, in areas like going back to work after a baby, the difficulties of child care, the challenges of premmie babies, and breastfeeding politics, that we thought the next wave of feminism and, indeed, social action, would be a motherhood movement. Basically, these gorgeous, like-minded women, from many different backgrounds and with many different experiences, felt mothers needed to be valued more.

In the spirit of this, I even did a newspaper interview about breastfeeding that I now am slightly embarrassed by (because I'm certainly no expert on it) but we had a mentor, Bridget, who was. A midwife and breastfeeding consultant, she helped us all during the wobbly early months; she inspired us to trust our instincts and be more confident.

We thought mothers had become so secure in their role, and the importance of respecting it, and supporting them, including their wellbeing and ability to work and be mothers, that some serious resources would be coming our way. (There's another book in how that panned out, and especially on the way parental leave and child care have become a political football in Australia.) I still keep in touch with, and just love, every one of those women back in Queensland. As good luck would have it, when I first had Clementine, I found a terrific midwife consultant named Anna, who was indispensable in those change-intensive days, though I'd very much have liked a mentor like Bridget too when I was bringing a new stepfamily together.

I found the discussions with women in my mothers' group about how we felt motherhood as an institution was travelling in Australia so stimulating that I got down to researching the wellbeing of children in my community. This included the concerns of parents who had kids with autism; the education needs of deaf children; parental involvement at school; migrant women making connections; women coming out of corrective institutions and their ability to move on; and those surviving family violence. I was interested in learning more about how we could all work together to support vulnerable people.

In 2015 I was asked to be on a discussion panel at the launch of Save the Children's report *State of the World's Mothers*. This was another turning point that galvanised my resolve to help mothers where I could. The panel included women leaders, an emerging scientist and a young mum who was an entrepreneur. In an era of mostly male-dominated panels, it was inspiring to hear about women's lives in Australia through a women-only lens—fancy that!

Save the Children also periodically reports on Australia's mothers and, while we routinely rank in the top ten internationally, within Australia there are key discrepancies when you look at each territory and state, and the factors in wellbeing. Mothers' health is measured by the number of doctor's visits they have while pregnant; children's health is measured by checking key areas of development; mothers' education is measured by the percentage of women who complete Year 12; and economic status is measured by average household income and mothers' access to social resources. Save the Children found that while most mums were doing well, Aboriginal and Torres Strait Islander ones were behind on almost all indicators and that mums in regional towns had less access to support. I was alarmed and thought this needed to change.

In other significant findings, Dr Cecily Strange, from the School of Population Health at the University of Western Australia, interviewed 300 mums who were connected with their community, had a lot of social contact and belonged to mothers' groups, and found links to mental wellbeing. (I wonder if there are stepmothers' groups?) In 2013 researchers at the University of Wollongong found a strong relationship between mothers' self-esteem and more satisfying relationships with their adolescent children.

It was as though I were back in childhood, sitting in a conference or on a living-room floor, listening to my mum and other women around me stand up for others in their community; the common bond, no matter their domestic arrangements, was mothering. I realised that not much had changed and this, and my second marriage, motivated me to concentrate more than ever before on families, particularly the wellbeing of mothers and children.

On the micro level of my own homefront, change was becoming our new normal by year five and each of us was learning to roll with it. I had returned to work in the mining engineering field with a public company. Bill had been elected parliamentary leader of the Labor Party after a turbulent period in Australian politics. Rupert and Georgette had started middle school, and the little one was starting to make friends and settle into new routines. Every so often, Clementine would come home and tell the big ones about her budding friendships; they were very encouraging and protective of their younger sister, without becoming 'little parents'. And the research shows that the kids from the earlier family usually have deep bonds but that these are unaffected by the introduction of a step or a half-sibling.

I encouraged Rupert and Georgette to read to Clementine and talk with her about what they were learning. They got into a pattern of comparing knowledge and facts, and loved to make her feel special by listening to all she could tell them about what she was learning. Encouraging the bonds between the kids has been my focus since year five, as the bonds they have with each of their three parents were already tight. With the two older ones going through the onset of adolescence at the same time as the youngest was starting school, I felt it was important to ensure they were valuing one another across the gulf of different ages and experiences.

There are steel-strong threads between the older two, who are only a year or so apart in age. Although, like all teenagers, they have their battles, it's them against the world every now and then. Once, I was remonstrating with Georgette about homework and whether she was applying herself at school, when she told me she wanted to be an actress when she grew up. I replied, 'Fine but you need to get good marks at school and go to uni first.' She was bereft, thinking I was telling her not to pursue her goals. My son overheard and, even though they were in the middle of their latest cold war, he stormed in and said, 'Don't you crush my sister's dreams!' Oops! Though I loved his ferocious defence of his sister.

By year five, the boundaries and communication methods in Rupert and Gigi's relationship with their dad had largely been established. The kids became accustomed to constant communication via phone, including FaceTime and texting, and their dad made regular visits and ensured he was with them for their special events, taking them to his Melbourne base. The three of them have their own rituals: finding restaurants together; doing, and going to, lots of sport; and adventures, such as sailing trips and learning to surf. By the fourth annual Dad–Rupert–Georgette snow holiday, Clementine had begun asking them if she could go next time and have their dad teach her how to ski.

Stepfamilies often negotiate school-holiday arrangements according to agreed rules, but by the year five mark, our arrangements had become more flexible. As parents, the three of us were getting into a rhythm just as the teenage years started to hit like a major weather event. We then needed to become more strategic about outings, discipline and expectations. This is a work in progress.

The relationship between my ex-husband and Bill is comfortable, but this kind of thing requires time and mutual respect. I've seen how delighted the kids are when Bill and their dad share a laugh or a funny story, and he was at the launch of Bill's 2016 federal election campaign. A cordial relationship between past and current partners is a balm.

As well, there were subtle, and not so subtle, signs the older children were adjusting well and putting down roots in their new home town. They'd started to say they were 'coming home' when they flew to Melbourne and started referring to local places and events that I didn't know about. When Bill and I looked at buying a house with a bit more space than our Victorian house, they were dead against it, imploring us to build another room on our existing place instead. They had become deeply attached to the little house to which we had all moved together as a new family unit. The older two children had very dear friendships with kids in the neighbourhood, feeling they had grown to know them so well, they would keep in touch 'for the rest of their lives'.

The kids' school reports and friendships were healthy and so were their bodies. But, keen to check further on their emotional wellbeing, I enlisted the support of a psychologist named Peter. I wanted some new tools to help them (and me) manage the kinds of things that political and public life throw at a family. Peter talked about the importance of time, and of Bill's relationship with the teens being close but not that of the bad cop (that's me). He was right. Researchers (Crosbie-Burnett and Giles-Sims, 1994) proposed that having a supportive stepdad who is 'high on warmth and low on control' is associated with the highest level of adolescent adjustment.

Still, I was juggling a lot, and perhaps putting too much pressure on myself when I felt I wasn't doing things 'well'. Full-time corporate work meant I was on call to attend to any issues or crisis management, which could mean phone calls at night, early morning teleconferences, and corporate functions (not to mention political ones when Bill was in parliament). As well, I had kids who went to school very early and a four year old who preferred twisting around in our bed to sleeping. I was also keenly aware of the importance of the obligations Bill had in his electorate, so would try to be with him for these.

I found a warmth of spirit in his women colleagues, from Queensland to Western Australia to Tasmania; they were welcoming and encouraging, inviting me to visit whenever I was in their electorates or to pop in with Clementine if I went to Canberra. I was touched, early on, when Tanya Plibersek, now the deputy opposition leader, dropped off at Bill's office a portable cot for us to use. I suspect Clementine's warm, starry-eyed attachment to Tanya stems from such stories of her support.

I was also very lucky to have made some wonderful friends in Melbourne. The women I was drawn to all had a natural inclination to support one another—whether they did or didn't have children, were sole mothers, career women or stay-at-home mums. I was shy about meeting people at first, but Bill kept introducing me to his friends, and I also met other women through the children's school, kindy and through work. I started to feel like I belonged. My anxiety also began to subside as I realised that, despite the transition, the kids were happy so far.

But, even though we as a family were feeling more consolidated, 2014 was a year of shocks. There were bushfires in Victoria, the terrible siege at the Lindt café in Sydney; as well, a spacecraft landed on a comet, 276 girls were taken from their school in Nigeria, ISIL started to make its horrific presence felt, it was the centenary of the Great War, and a passenger plane was shot down over the Ukraine. Also, Gough Whitlam passed away, and Australia looked back at the contribution he and his amazing wife, Margaret, made. I will always remember with gratitude the Whitlams' generosity of spirit when I was separating from my first husband, and sitting with them one afternoon when they were visiting my parents. We spoke about me focusing on parenting among other things, and they were kind, wise and without judgment.

In talking to the kids about marriage and remarriage, I consulted a range of sources, including the work of Martin Seligman, famed child psychologist. I aimed to avoid looking back in anger, even in tacit ways; and to highlight for the kids the lovely things from my ten-year first marriage: namely, them. Even when my communication with their dad has been wanting, I have talked to Rupert and Gigi about his total devotion to them and wheeled out anecdotes to reinforce the message. As the kids get older, they work out a lot of the family dynamics for themselves, and I let their interpretations unfold naturally. So long as they feel there is respect between all three of us adults, and that we have compassion for each other, that's the best I can do.

Among the statistics that show a higher divorce rate for second marriages is hidden the fact that many second marriages are happier than first marriages; and that they have many benefits after the first delicate years, when new couples aren't necessarily well supported and are experiencing major adjustment. If we treasured these families, and other non-nuclear families, a little more, we may prevent their feelings of culture shock and their potential breakdown, and create cushioning for the children, who deserve it.

In the *Journal of Family Psychology* report 'Families in Transition', the authors (Bray and Hetherington, 1993) state that once they are over the hurdle of those first few years, complex families can become even stronger: 'Although divorce and remarriage may confront families with stresses and adaptive challenges, they also offer opportunities for personal growth and more harmonious, fulfilling family and personal relationships.'

While more complex than first-marriage families, they are also intense and rich in experience, even as their needs are the same as those of all families.

New longitudinal research has brought new understanding of what goes right and wrong in stepfamilies. For example, that stepfamilies have a high rate of success in raising healthy children, with most of the kids not experiencing problems. These stepkids are resilient, and focusing on what makes them resilient creates opportunities for more kids in any kind of family to succeed.

We've learned it's not 'stepfamilyness' that is the source of problems for children, as such; rather, one of the main sources is conflict left over from the first marriage. Gender expectations about women's roles and responsibilities are at the root of some problems that develop in stepfamilies. However, largely due to the work required by them to adjust well, after five years stepfamilies are more stable than a lot of first-marriage families, and everyone in the family can experience real gains, particularly due to living in the environment of a happier relationship.

Ultimately, a stepfamily's ability to adapt to its changing environment depends on the relationships between the family members, and their larger network of family relationships (Minuchin and Fishman, 1981; Montgomery and Fewer, 1988).

For us, an added complication as we formed our new family was Bill's job, as it both put us in the spotlight and separated us for periods of time when he travelled to Canberra and around the country. All my life, I've watched wives, husbands and kids who are in public life, and noticed the kind of things they put up with, all in the interests of public service. I've seen women criticised for not being maternal enough; and men who have been heads of, for example, universities, charities and churches, who have suffered the slings and arrows of personal criticism because they are brave and visible.

I salute these community leaders every time they stand up for what they believe in, and I applaud their spouse, children or parents for their loyalty when someone tries to attack or humiliate these leaders for those beliefs, whether or not I agree with them. Tony Abbott's wife, Margie, for one, is a kind woman and dedicated mother. I found their bright, charming daughters to be unerringly polite and engaging, and whenever Margie and I were at public events together, she would generously always give me a tip on who was attending or show me where to sit.

While it's a deep privilege to serve your community, politics is a planet of its own, and the families of MPs at all levels of government, from all sides of the political spectrum, contribute an enormous amount of love to this country through the support they show its leaders and representatives. They may be stepfamilies, sole-parent families, same-sex-couple families, grandparent families, but the pressures of politics make for a stressful family life no matter what form your family takes.

When the kids first started to get into using technology to communicate with their family in Queensland and New South Wales, Skyping their dad in Brisbane became commonplace; it was a great tool, as they could control when and for how long they used it. Parliament, however, wouldn't enable them to have the technology on their computers, for security reasons. While I'm sure these were legitimate, I was amazed that more than a hundred families were unable to use this technology to keep those working in the capital in touch with the everyday things that make up the intimacy of family life.

That this is an environment that isn't looking to improve family solidarity any way it can is odd, considering how much our politicians invoke the sanctity of family, and tell stories about family. A sole dad I know tried to stay in political life, as a specialist in his advisory field, but couldn't get access to child care, so the country now misses his considerable expertise with him having gone back to the private sector. We should be doing more in this area, and learn from some of the processes that the Canadian and New Zealand parliaments, for example, have put in place to foster family ties.

I had been blessed to have help; without grandparents or siblings in Melbourne, I know I would have struggled through the past few years. Women have cared for me as well as for my kids: babysitters and teachers, who have been so generous and taught me so much about mothering—how far it stretches, the relentlessness of it, the fear you feel when you have a child. Those loving arms embracing my little ones felt like they were around me too. Kindy teachers, maternal-health nurses, midwives, childcare workers; these are my personal heroines, the fabric of my mothering, and the assuagers of my self-doubt. Hard-working, tolerant, funny and wise, these women have bustled in, bathed the kids, put on the dinner and tut-tutted at some of my decisions (not that I minded). If only every family going through a transition like ours could be so well supported; I am very conscious of the privilege of having access to help and never take it for granted.

I became interested in other stepfamilies living under the pressure of being in public life and discovered plenty of examples. The first US president had a stepfamily. George Washington married Martha Dandridge, a young widow who had two young children, Patsy and Jacky, then aged two and four. The Washington family were a warm, close unit. The story goes that when Patsy was gravely sick with tuberculosis, George nursed and sat with her, praying for her recovery. Jacky was by his stepfather's side in Yorktown when the British surrendered. As well, many more founding families of the US were stepfamilies due to death rates being higher in those days, and Barack Obama came from a stepfamily. Then there are all the sports stars, TV stars, writers, musicians, scientists, historians, doctors, clergy and jurists who have thriving stepfamilies.

In a bit of serendipity, I happened upon the work of an Australian academic living in New Zealand, Dr Claire Cartwright from Auckland University, and it spoke to me like no one else's. In one study she found that while researchers have investigated stepfamilies after remarriage, little is known about couples' preparation before cohabitation or remarriage. However, one US study asked stepfamily couples about their preparation for remarriage, and a more recent British study asked mothers and stepfathers about stepfamily life, with some attention to the period before repartnering. These studies suggest many couples didn't do much to prepare for stepfamily life. Many had repartnered quickly, and didn't discuss parenting and step-parenting roles before doing so. (Some parents repartner more quickly than they might otherwise have chosen to because of the difficulties of dating when they have children, and the financial burden of running two households (Cartwright, 2010).)

Talking about it all before you call the movers is so important— and not easy. How do you know what to expect? Cartwright really underscored for me how important it is for us as a community to support couples forming a family, whatever form it takes. This will then give us a body of knowledge that can operate as 'preventative maintenance' (to use a term from my days working in the resources area).

One thing that helps our family work is that, no matter how intense political life is, Bill and I make sure we always have an open dialogue about how we're all going. Also, we did a lot of work on the healthiest path to take in starting a stepfamily. Looking back over how our family developed, we have talked about what we did and didn't discuss before we got married, and what we would like to have known, including the kids' possible early-adjustment problems.

With the lack of examples for him to follow, Bill's relationship with his stepkids was based on his view that he was so blessed to have them in his life, he was just there to love them. I think the kids picked up on this quickly but, as I talked about earlier, it did make it tough for him to know when to step in—pun intended—regarding discipline. They were affectionate with each other, and had a lot of fun together. Sometimes it was like I was watching Bill live his childhood over again; they would have foot races and soccer games, and climb trees. All this gave me heart that, no matter what the 'deficit model' of stepfamily research says, we would be able to have something really solid.

It was, however, hard to know what to advise Bill to do if one of the kids was out of line, especially because he wanted to support me. He had to make it up as he went along, speaking quietly to them about whatever had happened, but leaving the rule-making and consequences to me. Over time, this changed, with him feeling more confident about reinforcing boundaries, and by the fifth year, Bill was coming up with some successful solutions to the perennial problem of disciplining children as a step-parent.

I learned from my stepfamily gurus (including Amato, Cartwright and Nicholson—sounds like a law firm, doesn't it?) that the step-parent can gradually adopt an authoritative parenting role with the child. So, it's important that step-parents take time to get to know their stepchildren and develop a relationship with them. It seems that if children come to care about their step-parent and feel cared for by them, they are more likely to grant the step-parent some authority. In other words, they will listen and pay attention to what the step-parent says, as opposed to saying, 'You're not my parent' (Schrodt, 2006). This pattern of high warmth and low control has been found to characterise functional stepfamilies; the less controlling and more laid-back the stepfather's relationship with the kids, the better (Ganong, Coleman, Fine and Martin, 1999).

Bill and I both try to ensure we are not 'parenting by feel', which is when we react before thinking it through, often just repeating our own experiences as children—an approach that doesn't always work today. Sometimes we can catch ourselves 'subconsciously parenting' and not thinking through exactly what the right reaction is to the particular situation. It's hard being mindful all the time! But when I wasn't on top of it, I felt terrible guilt, which I wouldn't have felt were we not a stepfamily. I felt that Bill supported me, but suspect he sometimes felt I wasn't making it clear what he should do or not do. When kids pick up on any sign parents aren't acting in harmony, they get confused or play up, and I didn't want Rupert and Gigi to blame Bill if I was seen to be supporting him in disciplining them. Tricky.

The glue that makes stepfamilies stick together is respect, according to the late Emily and John Visher, pioneers in the field of stepfamily advocacy and, for thirty years, in a stepfamily themselves. As well, psychologist Virginia Rutter, professor of sociology at Framingham State University in Massachusetts, tells us (1994):

> Both parents must require kids and stepparents to treat one another with respect. Only then can bonds between them develop. Despite feelings of jealousy and animosity, first and second spouses must also accord one another respect to accomplish the coparenting tasks the children need to do well. For their part, the kids also need each of the coparents to refer to the other parent with respect. Children are quick to pick up hints of hostility on either side. For them, hostility becomes an invitation to play the grown-ups off each other, and to imitate unkind behavior.

It's clear that one of the major challenges stepfamily couples face is the development of a parenting alliance between the parent and step-parent (Kinniburgh-White, Cartwright and Seymour, 2010). The thought of a parenting coalition would once have been unthinkable, to me, and for many whose marriages have ended due in part, to conflict over different parenting models, it would seem impossible. But, over time, it has been pretty successful for us. Both the kids' dad and their stepdad supported my decision-making, and we have learned to respect each other and stick together in the face of the enemy: the teens (just kidding!). When the kids started referring to having three parents, we felt we had really made progress.

Stepfathers who are supportive of both the kids and the mother help the family to become well adjusted; the studies show adolescents in well-adjusted stepfamilies benefit from and value supportive stepfathers for whom they have positive regard (Cartwright points to the research of Schrodt, 2006). Where there is less conflict, and mothers are more supported there are more good outcomes for the kids.

Claire Cartwright is one of a small number of PhD scholars in Australia and New Zealand studying stepfamilies, and is an acknowledged authority. She notes that stepfathers who are friendly with their stepchildren are less likely to make mothers feel torn between them and the children. The children's adjustment is helped by stepfathers accepting 'children's needs for a close relationship with the mother and the special bond between mothers and children (usually considered problematic in first marriages)'. When I read this paper out to Bill one night and got to the words 'it seems likely that the best choice a mother can make is to choose a stepfather who will be supportive of her and friendly toward her children', he said, 'Well you did that.' I did indeed. But I will keep reading the articles to him just the same.

7

When Mummy is okay

M Y MOTHER USED to say to me about motherhood, 'Look after yourself, because you're the centre of the family, and if you're not physically and emotionally well, everything else goes to pot.' Looking back, it's something I needed to do and didn't realise it as early as I should have. Mothers in a stepfamily, whether they're the biological mother or the stepmother, have additional responsibilities, and usually the inclination to be 'the nurturer', coupled with the desire to make everything run as smoothly as possible for the children. As well, gender-based expectations often mean the pressure becomes intense. Given that all the experts say mothers are the glue in a stepfamily, it makes sense to ensure that we are both well and well informed.

Claire Cartwright has looked at how mothers in stepfamilies use the internet to get information, noting that mothers' competent parenting in family transitions improves quality mother–child relationships and, in turn, has the biggest influence on how distressed the children feel. How dads cope will also impact on children and so they need specific knowledge too. As a consequence of my own experiences, I've become a loud supporter of quality accessible content (as opposed to odd advice!) for families, and hope that one day soon there will be plenty of expertise available online too, particularly to help those who are sole parents, lack mobility or live in remote areas. I can't imagine trying to do the (I hope) competent parenting I did when our family was undergoing big changes without advice from websites. Again, for women in regional areas, access to expertise can be challenging, so this channel is crucial to their ability to do their best.

I had great conversations with some of these mums during the federal election campaign, when I would be waiting for Bill in a hall or shopping centre, or after one of his talks. It was obvious from my discussions that the researchers (Weaver and Coleman, 2010) who found 'mothers in stepfamilies are faced with more complexity and have additional roles compared to their first married peers' are on to something.

Even when all the planets are aligned—with a strong marriage, resources, community support and the mother being physically and mentally healthy—mothering challenges us. When the kids are in a very emotional phase, and there is a new relationship to nurture and lots of uncharted territory to navigate, meeting everyone's needs can stretch you very thinly indeed. Doing it without running yourself into the ground is a hard one. How things unfold can depend on the age of the children; research suggests they are more adaptable to change the younger they are because critical thinking and the added angst of the teenage years have yet to kick in.

See the heavy lifting of creating a new family situation as a team effort, and make sure you are well supported by the people around you. I call these vital allies my 'floaties', because they are like those ever-popular inflatable arm cuffs you put on little kids to keep their heads above water in swimming pools. Your 'floaties' will include such experts as a good family therapist or counsellor, friends who offer emotional support, and the care you must extend to yourself.

Although educators and therapists advise mothers to proceed slowly (Hetherington and Kelly, 2002; Visher and Visher, 1988), some might feel unable to do this, and when mothers have made the decision to remarry, there is little evidence-based research to guide them in how to prepare children for the changes—as I found out by trying to locate some. So, mothers, 'the glue of the family', can find themselves in the position of making up their new role as they go. Research also shows many couples do little to prepare for living in a stepfamily, as many repartner quickly and do not discuss parenting and step-parenting roles prior to committing to the new partnership.

Resourcefulness is required to prepare the children for step-family life, manage the demands on the mother's time and attention, work through the impact of the step-parent role, and to be aware of parenting-coalition and loyalty issues. It is a massive transition to marry into an existing family unit and build a new marriage, and fostering the children's resilience and wellbeing, and coping with constant unknowns, takes enormous energy, strength and courage.

The Australian Institute of Professional Counsellors (AIPC) has some good advice: namely, deal with your own baggage first. Understand as much as you can about yourself, your childhood and the expectations you had, and have. This was helpful to me and is an ongoing process. The idea is to try to be aware of the impact on your family of past relationships and the process of divorce, and that you not try to recreate the past in a better version. The more the couple can work on addressing and calibrating these influences, the more successful the union is likely to be.

If you are taking children into a stepfamily situation via remarriage, counsellors advise that you undertake the process slowly, and talk a lot to the children about what is happening and about future plans. Cartwright's research tells us that once a couple has decided to commit for the long term, the more communication there is with the children, the more a part of things the children feel. This helps them feel less powerless at a time of uncertainty.

Longitudinal studies show that mothers have a lot of pressure on them at the beginning of the adjustment to stepfamily life and particularly at a time, Cartwright observes, 'when children are also at increased risk of adjustment problems'. You will be tempted to put the bulk of your day-to-day energy into maintaining the children's stability and happiness as they transition to the new situation. Expect to be pulled in plenty of different directions.

Some mothers appear successfully to navigate these challenges of divided attention and loyalties, and these issues might be largely resolved by the time stepfamilies are established (Hetherington, 1999). But we need deeper investigation of mothers' experiences raising children in stepfamilies. The AIFS warns us that, to date, we know little about the ways in which mothers successfully communicate to children about remarriage, manage the demands on their time and attention, work with step-parents and the children to support their step relationship, and manage loyalty issues with children as they arise. I would have loved to meet people in my new home town who could share their experiences, but it's a bit awkward if you're introducing yourself at parent gatherings by asking who there is part of a stepfamily!

Early in the formation of our new family unit, I was conscious of the need to carve out space to continue feeling connected to the older kids. When their dad and I parted ways, the three of us moved to a small townhouse that allowed the kids to feel physically closer to each other at a tough time. We created new ways of doing things together: lots of time at the playground up the road, me learning Rupert's favourite games and cooking the things they liked. Though my days were full to the brim, as were theirs, with the confusion of all the back and forth of living in two homes, we were able to grow closer by making the very most of our time together. I worked long days and was travelling for my job, but they would come to my office after school some afternoons (God bless my then employer's forward-thinking HR boss, who developed a family space for employees, years ahead of many other companies). I remember how time-poor and exhausted I was during that period but also the rare recalibration it gave me when it came to spending quality time with my children.

Experts know that the post-separation period is often a time the children have received more lax parenting, and that this is often one of the hardest parts of kids adjusting to a new person coming into the family—not getting away with as much! Still, there is some evidence that mothers when remarried might have difficulty maintaining focus on the children because of the demands, and perhaps attractions, of the new couple relationship.

In my case, the children were also competing for attention with a new baby sister. I had to be very disciplined with the precious time I spent with each of them, and even little things, like preparing the sandwiches they loved most or putting notes in their lunchboxes, sent the message that I was always thinking of them. (And occasionally I'd get a reply to the notes I left on the bathroom mirror.)

Mothers in stepfamilies also face complex loyalty issues, with some giving their loyalty to their children (Weaver and Coleman, 2010). On the other hand, some children perceive there has been a loss of loyalty through the mother's alliance with the stepfather (Cartwright and Seymour, 2002). Stepfamily therapists sometimes talk about the importance of adults having a 'united front', but children object if they think that parents are taking sides against them with step-parents (Cartwright and Seymour, 2002; Kinniburgh-White, Cartwright and Seymour, 2010). On the other hand, children notice and value it when their parents give them attention and make time for them after the stepfamily forms (Cartwright and Seymour, 2002).

When I remarried, I think the kids missed to some degree that time we spent as just the three of us. I made sure I had private time with each of them but, looking back, I think it would also have been a good idea to have allocated more time to the three of us. I chose not to because I was concerned not to make Bill feel left out—though, in retrospect, I am certain he would have understood and supported this. Since those early days, I have learned that keeping time and space for the original unit to spend time together is a useful 'adaptive tool'. But so little is out there to help imminent and fledgling stepfamilies prepare that a lot of women find themselves feeling their way in the dark, as I discovered when speaking to these women.

Family psychologists advise that if you are becoming the partner of someone who already has children and are becoming an overnight parent, avoid—to ensure the smooth running of the household routine—taking over roles the children may already have been performing. Don't step into the role of primary domestic organiser—as many women still think they should—rather, encourage the father to view this as a shared role. As the stepmother, and especially when the children's mum is still alive, you are not there to be the 'other mother' and run the household; you're there to support and be the kids' friend. You cannot afford to let the maternal instinct take over, as this can alienate the children and, most importantly, drain you thoroughly at an already demanding time. If necessary, you must teach the children and your partner not to expect you to fill that role, as it will not produce the healthiest outcome for any of you.

One US study showed that 'step-mothers experience greater difficulty with step-children than step-fathers do' (Nielsen, 1999). UK researcher Gill Gorrell-Barnes and others (1998) interviewed fifty adults who had grown up in stepfamilies and concluded 'adult step-children were much more judgmental of step-mothers', which may be due to the special importance given to the role of mothers (Nielsen, 1999). This can be exacerbated when residential fathers and their spouses choose to 'maintain traditional gender roles, with step-mothers taking over responsibility for the management of the household and the step-children'.

In an excellent Australian journal, *Family Matters*, Cartwright and her colleagues argued such studies support the importance of step-parents developing positive relationships with stepchildren before attempting to take on any type of parenting role (for example, Hetherington and Kelly, 2002; Papernow, 2006a; Visher and Visher, 1996). Papernow talked about the lack of a 'middle ground' in the step-parent–stepchild relationship in the early years of living as a stepfamily, and it seems likely step-parents would be more successful if they took the time to get to know their step-children, and demonstrated acceptance of them, gave them support and supported the biological parents' authority. Therefore, it seems that particular clinical and research attention should be focused on assisting step-parents who have an authoritarian style to adapt to, and cope with, the demands of step-parenting. (Cartwright, Farnsworth and Mobley, 2009).

So, traditional 'mum and dad' gender roles are not necessarily what works best for the step-parent. Biological parents, however, continue in their parenting roles, although there are a number of big adjustments in tandem with this. There will be a lot of expectations, and intense emotions, including grief (conscious and unconscious) over the lost ideal of the family, guilt about the marriage failing or sorrow about a parent dying; and this last scenario can lead to family members idealising the parent who is not there. Additionally, domestic roles, obligations from a previous marriage and financial setbacks from the cost of divorce all need to be factored in. Children can even feel guilty and disloyal if they begin to form a bond with the step-parent.

As well as the domestic and logistical load of running the new family unit, discipline and rule setting need to be a joint task. The step-parent is working on being friends with the children and building trust, and this can be undermined if they are carrying out the disciplinarian role. For example, it was potentially confusing when I would ask Bill, who hadn't been in a fatherly role before, to involve himself in problem solving but then get crabby if he disciplined the kids in a way I wouldn't have. Working out who does what, and when and how, takes time and lots of patience.

Research has shown that reasons for remarriage include economic incentives, wanting to have another pair of hands around the house, and companionship. For men bringing a new partner into an existing family unit, stepmothers can act as 'carpenters', repairing damaged relationships between the father and his children. A word of advice to fathers, however, is not to repartner as a means of being 'looked after' or having someone else look after your children. Women under thirty-five are likely to remarry, and women over forty are less likely to. Young mothers are likely to remarry, in the hope they can continue to build their family by having more children.

I heard Professor Matt Sanders, founder of Positive Parenting, on ABC radio, talking about stepmothers' experience as seen through research findings. He explained that they are generally thrust into the thick of family life faster than stepdads (by virtue of expectations that women will be maternal), and presumed to be ready and able to take charge of things like bedtime routines, nurturing and children's homework. Sanders pointed out that children need time to get used to you before you attempt to assume such a wide range of responsibilities and have such a sphere of influence in their lives. He stressed that it is important that you feel the children 'give you the authority' to do this, as 'it lets them have some power if they get to know you first'. The father must maintain responsibility for his children.

Sanders said the ideal role for new step-parents is one that is 'semi-parental at first'. When parents repartner, it is a signal to children that the former relationship is really over, killing the fantasy their parents will reunite, 'so this is a time to be gentle'. The potential new step-parent should be introduced gradually, and the children included in discussions about how family life will be run. Their cooperation cannot be demanded and affection must be earned. If a child is acting out, the response should be left to the biological parent. He suggested consulting a specialist psychologist if a child's behaviour is considered problematic.

Sanders also advised you aim to create a 'stable, predictable, comfortable environment' for the children, as this is ideal for all kids whatever their family situation. As a couple, be quick to seek help if you are having issues, as working it out together will give you the best chance of making it over the five-year hurdle. And constantly keep in mind that 'what's good for the children is generally what's good for the adults'.

It has been known for forty years that the support of extended family, such as grandparents, aunts and uncles, will assist a stepfamily to integrate and be a stablising influence. My parents have been a bridge-building team both with their own family and with our stepfamily relationships. They always encourage respectful communication, speak positively to the children about their parents, and let them know they are there for them. I've found this especially valuable as the kids grow into teenagers.

I'm so grateful for the close relationship I had with both my grandmothers, particularly when I was a teenager. One represented a nearby place of refuge, and the other was a source of tenacious support; they were both always in my corner, even when I was horrid. There is an old saying about the relationship between grandparents and their grandchildren: that they have 'an enemy in common'. In any case, when I was growing up, my grandmothers were always there if I needed an understanding ear. Watching my children with their grandparents and their step-grandmother, Ann, Bill's late mother, I am so pleased they have the same blessing of an alternative safe place to be. I am certain that this helped the children through the large number of changes they went through.

It was my father who, ever so gently, alerted me to the possibility I was overcompensating with the kids after my divorce and that they were getting away with misbehaving. I was rationalising it on the basis that they were hurt and needed time to heal but, in fact, I was rather at sea as to the right responses, purely because I was putting a internal lens of 'they're children going through divorce' over everything that happened. Eventually, though, my father's wise words and websites such as *Raising Children* and *Stepfamilies Australia* gave me permission to let go of this guilt and worry and regain my tough 'mummyness'.

It was a wrench for my parents, and the kids' aunts, uncles and cousins, when I moved Rupert and Gigi to Melbourne, as it certainly was for their dad, and for us. However, Bill's twin brother, Robert, and his wife, Karen, and their children were here, and becoming close to this new arm of the family gave the children—and me—a real sense of belonging. Robert and Karen have two great kids who are similar ages to ours. Karen is a Queensland girl too and, like me, right into family traditions and celebrations, and the importance of family generally. She is an Olympian host of family events, including of broader family, such as friends and neighbours; generous doesn't quite cover it. As well as being warm and enveloping, she has a razor-sharp wit, and has also kept a keen eye on our kids' activities since they arrived in Melbourne. She, in particular, has been a central ribbon tying us together as Shortens.

As my parents were living in Canberra, the kids were especially lucky to have Bill's mum, Ann, still going strong when we moved to Melbourne. The special relationship that developed between them resulted from the children's openness, and her accepting and generous spirit. She was immediately loving and kind to them both, having, like Bill, had an instant increase in her kin—me, Rupert and Georgette. When we visited her at her home, she would ask the children all about what was going on in their lives, the teacher in her often present—she showed them trees and flowers in the garden, and picked apples with them, as well as encouraging them to play with her big, old Corgi and talking to them all about books, of course. I encouraged them to think of Ann as a respected elder, and, as she was quite fascinating, this was easy. They learned that 'Panma', as Clementine dubbed her, had written books herself, and we have a copy of her published thesis, which is like a doorstop, at home. I have a treasured photo of her with the children on my desk and kept reflecting on it while writing this book. When Ann passed away, the children felt her loss acutely.

My belief that grandparents should be kept close by if you are lucky enough to have them was confirmed by a study by Dr Shalhevet Attar-Schwarz in the *Journal of Family Psychology* (2009), in which 1500 teens from 1000 schools were interviewed. It reported that—across all family structures—the more the teenagers talked to and got advice from a grandparent about social and school activities, or felt they could ask for money if necessary, the less hyperactive and disruptive they were. Kids with active relationships with their grandparents were more likely to get along with their peers; and, interestingly, adolescents in single-parent families and stepfamilies benefited the most, showing fewer behavioural problems and better social skills, particularly after divorce had occurred: '[grandparents] can reduce the negative influence of parents separating and be a resource for children who are going through these family changes'.

For those families who do not have the benefit of a close relationship with grandparents, including where the parents are in conflict with, or detached from, their own parents (or they are deceased), it can be helpful for the wellbeing of both younger and older people to form cross-generational friendships. I have 'borrowed' a grandmother from another family in my street, and I don't know what I would do without her.

Essentially, we all need as much support as possible, especially if we are sole parents. In my neighbourhood, of St Lucia, three of my best friends were being raised solely by their mothers. It didn't seem unusual but I guess, as a four year old, it didn't occur to me that it was. And in the 1970s in Brisbane, the statistics were not as they are today. In Australia in 2016 we have 1.1 million sole-parent families, 80 per cent of which have a female parent and 20 per cent of which have a male parent. The ABS projects that by 2036, there will be more than 1.5 million sole-parent families. The reasons behind these figures are wide ranging: from the incidence of divorce (which, however, seems to have plateaued in the past few years), to unplanned pregnancies, to more people choosing to have a child alone. In whatever way sole-parent families have been formed, we need to find optimum methods to support their functioning and equilibrium, especially given their growing numbers.

Women are increasingly choosing to have children alone, which is a product of their growing economic independence. The process of choosing this path is liberating for some and less easy for others. Either way, it's certainly not without its challenges.

Whatever the social reasons—and there are many and various— in Australia the average age of first-time mums is now twenty-nine.

While I was in my first professional job, and actually responsible for people and budgets, I met a woman my own age who was smart, sassy and hyper organised. I admired her direct style, and learned some of her techniques for managing in a world of men. Fiercely professional, she managed always to be unruffled and punctual, so I was surprised to learn she was a single mum, even though I would never have thought of my childhood buddies' mothers that way. One day, bristling at being addressed with this term at work, she turned to the group and said, 'Sole parent, actually; whether I'm single or dating or married isn't relevant.' Despite it, though, I cringe at the thought of how tone deaf I was, and sometimes reflect on how much she had to compensate as a lone parent in a male-dominated company where meetings, and teleconferences with people throughout the world, were scheduled at all hours of the day or night long before flexible arrangements became commonplace. Since then, I've tried in the workplace to be aware of people's responsibilities and the subtle messages in the language we use when talking about them—let alone when we call meetings. I haven't always been afforded the same courtesy, though. The words we use are important and, in my experience, this isn't just about political correctness but also thoughtfulness.

Over the past few decades, there has been much discussion of how children of sole-parent families get on in life. With increasing numbers of families becoming sole-parent households, again partly as a result of society's growing acceptance of divorce, they are usually headed by mothers, as Jennifer Baxter from the AIFS reports.

Throughout history, most sole-parent families resulted from the death of a partner (often of the woman, in childbirth), and remarriage was a financial necessity (for a widow) or a practical necessity (for a man left with children to look after). So, again, stepfamilies have always been with us, and many of them have been an ongoing support for parents and children who would otherwise have been without it.

While there is evidence internationally that children from such families can have poorer outcomes than those from two-parent families, and this is a concern, the reasons why are under-researched (Amato and Sobolewski, 2001). Why kids slip up is more likely to do with what's happening in their family than what type of parents they have. Parenting practices, economic circumstances and parents' mental wellbeing have been identified as factors, just as they have in nuclear families.

Professor Jan Nicholson is leading research into the effects of living in sole-parent families as well. She's discovered that while children who are raised in sole-parent families and in stepfamilies usually fare more poorly across a range of areas, such as behaviour, social skills, scholastic performance and emotional wellbeing, than those from stable two-parent families, these outcomes are mostly associated with family instability. And when children undergoing similar amounts of adversity are compared, the family structure makes very little difference (Nicholson, Fergusson and Horwood, 1999). However, as Nicholson writes:

There are a whole lot of changes associated with family breakdown that make this a really challenging time for mothers.
When you combine this with financial strain—and in Australia,
we have extremely high rates of poverty that affect single
parent families—children are exposed to a range of circumstances that have adverse impacts on their development: change
and unpredictability spanning multiple environments (family
breakup often results in moving house and possibly schools,
loss of some family and social networks), a mother who is
working longer hours and less emotionally available because
of what she is going through, lax and inconsistent parenting,
and heightened conflict between separating parents—this
can be a pretty toxic combination for children if it persists
over time.

I still recall from my own short time as a sole parent the exhaust-
ing juggling and constant need to draw on all my resources and
strength, and that was with the blessings of economic independence, an occupation I loved, supportive friends and family. I often
wonder how parents on their own who are without these resources
manage to do such an amazing job. Because many children in sole-
parent families don't, of course, have impaired outcomes.

Personally, I know several people—a man and a number of
women—who are raising children alone. Each of them is a completely dedicated parent, and the children are greatly loved and just
like the other children we know who have two parents. We are
involved in each other's lives, and I'm sure this joint effort protects
all of us.

The lovely Agnes is eleven years old, the unplanned, but dearly
desired, daughter of a close friend of mine, who, just like me,
had planned on marriage and pregnancy. Aged thirty-six, having

been married and divorced, she thought she would never have a child. When she became pregnant, she decided to raise her baby alone. Perhaps she wasn't really alone, though: her mother has been a constant parenting support, and her dearest friends are her neighbours, who are daily features in her daughter's life. My friend and I talk about parenting a lot, and especially about community support. I know her delightful neighbourhood friends well and she knows mine. She told me, 'While I have received support from my friends—in terms of child care, predominantly—I believe this is because I have an incredibly supportive and established community who care, rather than because I'm a sole parent.' The thing that strikes me is not just her dedication as a parent, but the reserves she has and her wise perspective.

When I asked her about the stereotyping of sole parents (especially mothers), she said: 'I didn't experience any other blended or sole-parent families, that I know of, in any of the three significant communities in which I grew up—church, school, or neighbourhood—all very white, middle-class settings. I am surprised that I haven't experienced any stigma from others associated with my chosen family form. The key contributor to any stigma is me.' Hearing that made me feel a pang of sadness.

Agnes was in full-time private child care from the time her mum returned to work until she started school. It was then that her grandmother, at age seventy, decided to retire from full-time employment to assist with before- and after-school care. This has continued and now, more like what goes on in the vibrant migrant families in Melbourne than the usual practices of an Anglo family, her grandmother lives part of each week in Agnes's home.

'I really cannot provide advice for grandmothers in a situation such as mine, except to say that if they choose not to embrace their daughter and her child, they will miss out on the privilege and joy of having a grandchild, and the ongoing pleasure of a relationship with both mother and child. This joy is my experience but I am aware that life does not always follow this pattern,' Agnes's grandmother told me.

I've heard grandparents announce they are just in love with their grandkids. 'All care and no responsibility!' they say, 'we just spoil them and give them back.' Sometimes it's more complicated than that, though.

Divorce or the death of a parent can mean grandparents are suddenly thrust into a more intensive role with their grandchildren, and during a time of great change and stress. On the other hand, changed family circumstances can also mean a sudden decrease in their involvement with their grandchildren. Stepfamilies Australia advises that most step-grandchildren consider the step-grandparent relationship important; they are eager for more contact with step-grandparents and to maintain this relationship as they get older:

> Communication with the parents of the grandchild is essential in the initial stages, as they may need you in a different capacity than before. They may be particularly sensitive to criticism or your opinions as a result of the changes in family. Accept that the new family formation as it changes and extends all takes time to settle and there will be a role adjustment for everyone involved.

While the 'family decline' hypothesis assumes the primacy of the nuclear-family model of two biological parents, family sociologist Vern Bengtson, from the University of Southern California, argues that family relationships across several generations are becoming increasingly important in American society. They are also increasingly diverse in structure and in their functions. This opinion is also held by experts in Australia and other countries. The nature of stepfamilies gives children the opportunity to gain more kin, and more support resources, such as step-grandparents.

Demographer Peter McDonald (1992) has written a terrific overview of the extended family in Australia. In it, he says there is great benefit in the support from these kin, especially for those who are vulnerable, isolated or aged, or young homeless people. In his words, 'we should re-evaluate the importance in our society of family relationships beyond the boundary of the household'. He says the evidence doesn't support the assumption we aren't as close to our extended family and that, in fact, the growth of cities and increasing use of cars may have led 'to families these days being closer together than they were in the past'. McDonald and others found that extended family, and especially grandparents and step-grandparents, can help make kids in stepfamilies feel protected. I could not agree more. My kids have such a sense of being 'grandchildren'; they have grandparent time, sleepovers, secrets and stories, photos on their mobile phones, as though my parents were living in the same suburb as us.

The National Stepfamily Resource Center advises:

Since grandparenting relationships can be extremely important to the welfare of the grandchildren, the efforts of grandparents to maintain and enrich bonds are certainly worthwhile. The support of grandparents can be invaluable as children face adjustments to new family situations and are dealing with feelings of uncertainty and loss. Remember that although you need to separate from your former spouse, your children very much need to continue both parental and extended family relationships. Encourage your children to maintain close ties with their biological grandparents.

Bengtson (2001) conducted research based on one of the largest studies of its kind in the world, the US *Longitudinal Study of Generations*, to demonstrate the strengths of multigenerational ties over time, and why it is necessary to look beyond the nuclear family when asking whether families are still functional. For children in stepfamilies, these intergenerational relationships are the ties that help them through the transition. Bengtson argues multigenerational relationships will be more important in the twenty-first century for three reasons: the demographic changes of the population ageing, resulting in 'longer years of shared lives' between generations; the increasing importance of grandparents and other kin in fulfilling family functions; and the strength and resilience of intergenerational solidarity over time.

I applied Bengtson's findings to my own family, which includes a few only-child families, and realised that extended-family ties are crucial and cherished. Both my parents and their parents fostered a sense of the importance of such ties, and second and third cousins on both sides of our family trees are still in touch. Recently, Bill's and my children have gotten to know his cousins and their children, and formed new friendships of surprising intensity. I adore them too; they were an unexpected bargain that came with our marriage.

Also, with so many single parents now empty-nesters, extended family is a reliable support. What was once an inverted-pyramid to depict nuclear-family history (with the children at the bottom) is increasingly thinner, in what some researchers call the 'beanpole effect'. We are going to live longer lives with fewer offspring, so the extra family members will be welcome.

Perhaps we could look to the Chinese, who have a unique and ancient family model based on deep respect for their elders. It is still common, despite the one-child policy, to find four generations living under one roof, looking after each another.

The two chief maxims from my childhood and motherhood are 'It takes a village to raise a child' and 'When Mummy is okay, the whole world is okay.'

Indeed.

8

The upside
(is in the research)

I ASKED BILL WHAT were some of the key things he had learned from our research that rang true after seven years living in a stepfamily. While saying that he wished he'd had access to the research earlier, even though it needs 'to be put into plain English', his response was simple but, no doubt, echoed that of many people who enter stepfamily land without a map (as, indeed, most do). 'Be their friend first' were the words that resonated most with Bill, as a loving man who went, as he says, 'From zero kids to three'.

There is a growing body of international research available on how stepfamilies fare, and thrive, in the longer term, though, as Bill also pointed out, the positive information about stepfamilies is more difficult to find than evidence about why they may not do as well. In other words, the good news for stepfamilies is much harder to find than bad news and negative stereotypes of stepfamilies.

Having spoken to so many stepfamilies, and having read so much about the nature of the stepfamily—and especially the fact that it does not need to try to operate identically to a typical nuclear family to be just as happy and functional—there are many things Bill and I put into practice. The knowledge that everything can be changed and roles may not be as fixed as in a nuclear family has been very useful, as has the understanding there may be times we need to revisit the earlier of Patricia Papernow's stages of stepfamily stabilisation (2006b).

Reading so much about stepfamilies, and how individuals within them do best, has boosted my confidence in my own parenting. I am also more sure about Bill's and my commitment, and ability, to co-parent and respond to challenges as a united force. I feel better informed, and more confident about ceasing much of the overcompensating I was doing to try to ensure the children were not disadvantaged by becoming part of a stepfamily, rather than remaining in a nuclear one.

Hillary Clinton wrote that every child needs a champion and someone to believe in them no matter what they do, and as I was reading that, I realised that Bill is that for Rupert. Bill has really become his champion; he will, when I'm being pretty tough on the kids or not necessarily seeing something from their point of view, often come to me later and give me a slightly different perspective. He doesn't say to the kids, 'I'm going to go and represent you,' he just quietly puts their case. Having read so much about how step-parents need to find roles in the new family that are fruitful for them and the children, I agree with the researchers who say that being the child's friend first is a great approach, and I would add that 'the children's champion' is a good way for them to think of themselves.

Another insight Bill gleaned from our reading on how to approach step-parenthood was to be patient. 'You don't have to try to be their parent and disciplinarian; instead, first be their friend and don't rush anything. Don't rush to judgment, and don't rush to be hard on yourself,' he says; also, 'Don't lecture, show children what you expect by example.'

Bill and I also learned that when striving to form a harmonious stepfamily, looking back at your own childhood in a solid nuclear family, with defined and traditional parental roles, will not necessarily provide the most useful template. 'Don't put unrealistic pressure on yourself or your kids—or your partner—to be perfect,' was one of the most useful messages we received from what we read.

Also, perhaps most importantly of all, Bill recalls the following as being a vital piece of expert advice: 'You've got to give it time, nothing in stepfamily building and reinforcing happens without time.' He advises other men entering into stepfamily life without having yet had children of their own to 'Ask for help, ask questions and don't think you're stupid—there's a lot of knowledge out there among other dads; you've got to ask.' I've come to understand that it's more productive to regard mistakes you make in good faith not as failures, as I would previously have regarded them, but as signs of progress. This is something I've learned both through our seven-year-plus stepfamily journey and through my reading. In hindsight, though I feel I let Bill down by not better helping him prepare for instant stepfamily-hood (despite the fact I am such a 'preparation' person), it does feel like any mistakes we made were, in fact, part of our development.

On balance, while local and international research has long found stepfamilies to be more fragile than families of first marriages in the two years after their formation, there is also a lot to make us take heart. Once stepfamilies establish themselves, they can have much to teach all types of families.

In fact, some researchers question if the shakiness of stepfamilies in the early days is more due to our culture's lack of support for non-nuclear family models than it is to the family's type. Dr Virginia Rutter is one who believes stepfamilies have qualities from which all families could learn, saying the best available research shows 'contrary to myth, stepfamilies have a high rate of success in raising healthy children [in the US study by Hetherington] 80 per cent of kids come out fine' (1994). With hundreds of thousands of Australian kids living in poverty, we should seriously question if it's the structure of non-nuclear families that causes hardship, or if poverty is the crucial factor we should be looking at.

Rutter also points out that stepkids are resilient and that study-ing their resilience—not just focusing on their problems—could help kids who belong to any kind of family. Again, the problems that affect stepchildren have less to do with being in a stepfamily and more to do with conflict: parental conflict left over from the first marriage can be one of the biggest sources of their problems, she writes (1994).

Long-term research is now showing the specific problems that these families may encounter, rather than continuing to work from 'deficit model' comparisons based on the first six months of stepfamily adjustment, which made their issues sometimes seem insurmountable. There have been findings that after five years, stepfamilies can be more stable than families of first marriages; this is because second marriages can be happier than first marriages, as people are more experienced, mature and know themselves better by the time of a second marriage. In her article 'Lessons from Stepfamilies', in the US journal *Psychology Today*, Rutter says stepfamilies experience the most trouble in their first two years, before levelling out. They are not just 'make do households limping along after loss', and 'All members experience real gains, notably the opportunity to thrive under a happier relationship' (1994).

As I see it, the needs of people in stepfamilies are no different from those in any other family: to have autonomy over their lives, to belong to a family, to have attachments, and be loved and cared about. According to Paul Amato, while the average child in a stepfamily may not be doing as well as the average child in a nuclear family, studies show that 40 per cent of children in stepfamilies are doing better than children in nuclear families.

The key reasons why some children in stepfamilies may have less chance to thrive than those in nuclear families, according to Hetherington's 20-year longitudinal study of post-divorce families at the University of Virginia (Hetherington and Kelly, 1993), are as follows. While some kids in post-divorce families may experience depression, have lower academic performance or engage in delinquency at some time, it is often a response to the reduction in their parents' attention when they are recovering from a divorce, starting a new marriage, and distracted by the new relationship and adjusting to their change in lifestyle. Some of these children will be adjusting to a parent being absent from their lives altogether.

Hetherington underscores that children whose parents remarry are not doomed: in fact, 80 per cent are not recorded as having behavioural problems. So, again, despite the fact children in stepfamilies seem to be at greater risk of adjustment problems, most of them are doing fine. Hetherington shows between two thirds and three quarters of children in stepfamilies (and this is even higher if the child is living in a well-established stepfamily) do not exhibit serious emotional or behavioural problems. In the long run, 'the response of most children to the challenges of stepfamily life seems to be characterized by resiliency and adaptability' (Arnold, 1998). She calls for more studies on the strengths of these families and the resilience of the kids themselves.

In 'It Was the Best of Times, It Was the Worst of Times', Bridget Freisthler and others (2008) conducted in-depth interviews with thirty-six young-adult stepkids about their experiences, and perceptions of the best and worst of stepfamily life. The paper was designed to elicit what they thought, rather than what the research showed them to be 'at risk' of. They identified three benefits acquired from being in a stepfamily after divorce: emotional resources, material resources and personal growth. The 'worst' aspects of the stepfamily experience were emotional stress; divided loyalties between the two families; loss; change; and the step-parent not really being a parent.

I wonder how these experiences would compare to the best and the worst in life in any nuclear family, especially one in an unhappy state? All families have their best and worst of times, and, as Leo Tolstoy wrote in *Anna Karenina*: 'Happy families are all alike; every unhappy family is unhappy in its own way'. This has become shorthand to say that happiness relies on a number of factors but unhappiness can result from just one. So, it's the functioning of a family that will determine its happiness:

> Despite society's difficulty in accepting family diversity, research indicates it is not the form of the family that leads to problems for children, but it is conflict in the family that can produce lasting emotional difficulties. The family's task is to create emotionally supportive interactions within the family, regardless of family type. (Visher and Visher, 1995)

In 2013, the Household Income and Labour Dynamics study (HILDA) surveyed stepfamily happiness, and found 58 per cent of stepkids gave their satisfaction level as between eight out of ten and ten out of ten. Only 20 per cent of respondents rated it as five or less out of ten. As with any type of family, external factors (such as being born during wartime), the ages of the children, the ability to communicate well, the levels of conflict, and the individuals themselves, determine a family's functioning and adaptation. And the experts are, of course, telling us that for every real pitfall of stepfamily life upon which a myth is built, stepfamilies in fact 'offer a positive opportunity in return' (Rutter, 1994). According to the study in 'Families in Transition' by Bray and Hetherington (1993), 'although divorce and remarriage may confront families with stresses and adaptive challenges they also offer opportunities for personal growth and more harmonious and fulfilling family and personal relationships'.

We know stepfamilies can be complex, diverse and intense. We also know that the lessons they, and other non-nuclear families, learn are valuable for all families. In preparing to repartner or in choosing to parent alone, or in a same-sex couple or, indeed, within a nuclear family, parents must be astute, conscious decision-makers, constantly learning, and flexible, thoughtful and communicative.

One significant change is that having kids today can be a more deliberate choice than it was in the past. These days, fathers are often older, and more active and not content just to be the wage earner or the authority figure in their child's life. There is also the stepfather who is eager to be a more involved parent than he was to his first set of kids, with a new partner who expects him to play a more equal role.

Claire Cartwright suggests that modern society should find clear roles for step-parents, to help them adjust more easily to the new household through giving them a strong sense of where they stand and what is expected of them. She cautions against fantasising about the way families should be, based on an idealised nuclear-family model. 'People who go into a remarriage with idealised and romanticised views of the family they are forming should review their expectations, and should not try to just recreate their nuclear family,' she said when I interviewed her for this book. Glorifying an often-unattainable ideal family state reinforces negative stereotypes about other family models.

Another leading scholar of families, Professor James H Bray, examined the factors that can predict a stepfamily's success, in a nine-year study of 200 first-marriage families and stepfamilies in Texas designed to pinpoint key factors in the development and solidification of stepfamilies. In his book *Stepfamilies: Love, Marriage, and Parenting in the First Decade* (1999), Bray writes that, although stepfamilies are assaulted on all sides by difficult and often divisive questions, the majority of step-parents remarry with optimism and new resolutions for a better life. He also writes about how loving, functional stepfamilies can lessen the trauma of parental divorce, and restore a child's and the family's sense of security; and how a stable stepfamily is as capable as a nuclear family of nurturing the healthy development of children, by imbuing values, setting boundaries, and providing a structure in which rules for living a moral and productive life are transmitted, tested (that is, rebelled against) and ultimately affirmed.

I feel the formation of a bond between a step-parent and step-child is like 'layering' a friendship: that is, building layer after layer of connections, rather than acting as through you're their teacher. In my experience, beginning life as a new stepfamily is similar in many ways to beginning life as a new parent, be it as the mother or father. When you are bringing home a new baby, there's a whole range of approaches you could take and they're almost the same ones as you'd take forming a stepfamily. It's all so new, you really don't have any idea what you're doing (though I hope this book goes some way to giving clues); there's a lot of ambiguity about rules, and mixed messages about what you should do; there are other people's expectations to factor in. If we looked at stepfamilies that way, they would be better supported in the community, I think.

Stubborn perceptions that stepfamilies rank well below nuclear families as ideal models in which to raise children are definitely a hurdle for those entering into stepfamilies with all the goodwill in the world to create a loving, stable and very fruitful environment for everyone in the new family unit. Bill says that much of what we read, or see, about stepfamilies continues to be 'disaster reporting' and he was quite surprised to learn there is a growing body of work showing the positive aspects of non-nuclear families. We, as a society, need to create pathways by which stepfamilies can seek support without thinking that, by doing so, they're admitting defeat or that as a family they are 'less than' anybody else.

What some people appear to have forgotten, or not to have known in the first place, is that the idea of what constitutes an authentic family has changed dramatically over time, just as it continues to evolve, and that families are also agents of historical change. The actual term 'nuclear family' only appeared in the early twentieth century, referenced by the *Oxford English Dictionary* in 1925, and established the label of a family being a household with a father, mother and their children living together. As American anthropologist George Murdock described it in 1949: 'The family is a social group characterized by common residence, economic cooperation and reproduction. It contains adults of both sexes, at least two of whom maintain a socially approved sexual relationship, and one or more children, own or adopted, of the sexually cohabiting adults.' On the other hand, *The Family: A World History* (2012), by Mary Jo Maynes and Ann Waltner, comments:

> The evolution of family life continues to shape and be shaped by historical forces. Now more than ever these changes take place in a global framework. The deep history of the family—reaching back to the earliest emergence of the human species—has left its imprint on global historical processes. Humans everywhere descend from common ancestors who evolved in the social context of domestic relationships.

I've found, to my surprise, that even definitions of nuclear families are not consistent. Some only allow it to include biological children that are full-blood siblings, while others allow for a step-parent and any mix of dependent children, including stepchildren or adopted children. The nuclear-family structure of one married couple and their children became the standard in Western Europe and New England in the seventeenth century, fostered by the church and theocratic governments. Then, with the emergence of early industrialisation and capitalism, it became the 'financially viable social unit'. However, it is now also suggested that nuclear families in England can be traced as far back as the Christian revolution in the fourth century (McDonald, 1992).

Since the 1950s, the nuclear family's dominance in modern society has been promoted by social conservatives called familialists. Familialism views the nuclear family, with one father, one mother, and their child or children, as the central unit of a functioning society and of civilisation. Familialism typically suggests that normality resides in the patriarchal nuclear family, usually opposing other social forms such as sole- or same-sex parenting.

However, in the United States the nuclear family has been challenged as being sociologically inadequate to describe the complexity and reality of family relations. Scholars argue that there has been much diversity in families since the 1950s, and that we shouldn't gloss over the reality that even in nuclear families, there can be exploitation and conflict. In the year 2000, nuclear families, including original biological parents, constituted roughly 24 per cent of American households. Approximately two thirds of all children in the US are expected to spend at least some time in a single-parent household. In the UK, the number of nuclear families fell from 39 per cent of households in 1968 to 28 per cent in 1992. According to Edwards (1991) and Stacey (1996), 'the nuclear family no longer seems adequate to cover the wide variety of household arrangements we see today'.

In Australia, although family is still considered the fundamental unit of society, much beneath its formal superstructure is evolving. Young adults more commonly delaying marriage, couples preferring to cohabit rather than marry, more women working after having children (so changing the 'traditional' family model of a working father and a mother at home with children), people having children later, declining fertility and the increasing divorce rate have all been identified as influencing the shape of what we think of as a family. The rigid concept of who qualifies as living in a true 'family' has altered irretrievably.

Given this, what is needed is a cultural shift to embrace non-nuclear families, including the way they are discussed, public policy and media representation. We should be saying that families come in all shapes and sizes, are all equally valuable, and deserve equal respect and support. Bill told me, 'When I look at the MPs I have in my team—single mums, step-parents, nuclear families, gay couples with kids—they all want the same thing for their kids, and that's what we've got in common: let's try to do the best possible parenting. They all want their kids to be better off than they were, that is hard-wired into the DNA of parents, and that impulse isn't determined by the nature of your relationship and who is in it, and who is not. The determination to make sure kids are better off is the common ingredient.'

He also made the excellent point that family research needs to be broader, bigger and deeper, to take in the massive demographic changes of the last decade. 'We need a much better-informed community about these things, blowing away the cobwebs of the stereotypes; really good research is absolutely critical,' Bill says.

Overall, the research I've studied suggests the modern family is dynamic, and changes according to the bigger global trends, including industrialisation, women's growing economic independence and their ability to depart unhappy marriages, and no-fault divorce. There is no sign these trends are reversing. As well, globalisation, economic shifts, poverty, unemployment, migration, mobility and education all affect the way families work and live. Just as step-families were once more common as a result of women dying in childbirth, or men dying at war, stepfamilies are becoming more common today due to a different wave of change propelled by factors experienced around the world.

In his article 'Extended Family In Australia', Peter McDonald notes that marriage and nuclear families are part of an ideal, and reflect the moral or ideological views of the time. However, with all the changes we face, we can't hang onto the nuclear-family model too tightly. In her assessment of family relationships in the UK, Finch (1989) said, 'The idea of the golden age in which family relations were stronger than they are today is clearly a myth, without foundation in its historical evidence.'

We need to be open to those who would thrive within a more extended model—sole parents; aged people; immigrants (like me!); young, homeless people; working mums at home.

Some families will define who is kin and who isn't based on things like who comes to Christmas dinner, who is asked to help with emergency child care, who is invited to a funeral, who is an emotional support in a crisis, and who you expect to help if you were in financial difficulty. There are also inclusions in, or exclusions from, who we think of as family based on what the law tells us—and perhaps on what our cultural history asks of us.

A few years ago, I visited the Kimberley and met a bunch of wonderful indigenous middle-school kids. Conversations are always tentative when you're an adult talking with teenagers but I found conversation with these young Aboriginal women to be even more tentative than usual. They were socially shy, and yet, when I was observing them before we sat together on a verandah and kicked our legs in the sunshine, they were very much in charge of themselves and their space. We talked about my family, and especially my youngest one, and I asked the names of some of the little children in the distance who were playing by a waterhole. We were sitting by a pond; it was a very hot, dry day. One little boy was enamoured with my boots, which had a small Cuban heel and came to mid calf. I slipped them off, and he put them on and was very pleased with himself. He clomped off, asking me to come with him to see the big old Brahman bull in the paddock. One of the young women suddenly looked at me and said, 'I only call him my half-brother to new people, but he's just my brother—cute in't, he?!'

Then they regaled me with information about their kin and clan connections. It was a maze, like those of royal Habsburg and the Battenberg families, and it was very clear their definition of kin was linked to their community and their history, and was much broader than mine. We spoke about hopes and dreams; we talked of life at school, and how much better it was to be at school on their country, in their neighbourhood. How their parents were relieved they were getting an education, from science and the arts, to animal husbandry, to language and technology. I asked about the cattle country, and what they'd tell a Queenslander who was accustomed to being around sheep about raising Brahmans, and then we talked hip-hop and rap lyrics, and Miley Cyrus. They were entrancing and clever.

I'd been asked to make a short speech that day, but what I'd prepared flew out the window as I sat in the usual row of plastic chairs where invited guests are plonked, on a little deck in the sun.

I looked out over the open faces of the parents, grandparents, aunties and uncles, teachers, elders and students, down on the grass, in rows of folding chairs. All I could think about was the closeness of these families—how they all knew each other, and where everyone was at any time; even the littlest one in the too-big boots. I imagined what it would be like to send my daughters thousands of kilometres away to school, when my entire world was my daily family life. I saw how everyone there seemed to feel a sense of belonging, and wondered if I could do what those families did for their children.

So, I ditched my notes and talked about what I knew. About moving away from what's been your place; about how it takes courage to send your kids anywhere, but especially if they are moving away from family, where they belong. Later, some of the parents, aunts and grandparents spoke to me, and one gave me a small gift, of a decorated pod from a boab tree, that I treasure. Every time I see it on my coffee table, I'm reminded that it's children themselves who really define who is family to them, and we should not try to shape that to fit our view of things.

The nuclear family has been around for as long as history has been recorded, and will endure in its current robust form. But none of the evidence suggests the rise of diverse family models threatens it in any way.

9

I wish I'd known then what I know now

Now that my two older children are teenagers, fourteen and fifteen, we know the equilibrium in the household will change. As they transition from child to adult, I'm sure we will find ourselves revisiting some of the stages of stepfamily evolution, and we're open to doing so. If there is one thing we've learned, it's that openness and flexibility need to be bywords for an evolving family.

Our kids are bright, curious and interested in questioning everything the adults around them propose. Although there have been many questions from their quarter, at the dinner table, or late at night, when we tend to talk before going to sleep, not many shockers have come my way. They have asked a bit about Bill's and my first marriages and weddings, and about our relationships when we were young adults. Our answers have sometimes forced them to put their fingers in their ears and go, 'Lalalalalalala,' so we know everything is as it should be, given that all teens do this to their parents at some stage.

In answering our children's questions about our new family, I have explained there are many reasons people remarry. I've told them that at one time people remarried to ensure financial security, or to gain a replacement parent for their children, and that, in those cases, remarriage was considered a necessity. I didn't remarry for those reasons, but because of the love I feel for Bill and what we would be able to create as a family. It was an optimistic thing to do, and I think it's like all great tales of hope and triumph!

A teenager has to start to broaden their sources of approval, away from their parents and towards their peers, so that they can establish their own identity. This is called 'individuating'. They also begin to think more deeply about everything, which heralds the move into adulthood. This, I have found, also means they rethink and question everything. I have done my best to learn what we should be telling them about marriage, divorce and remarriage, so they are able to develop a well-informed and healthy perspective to apply to their own future relationships. Sometimes I feel like we are now under serious scrutiny from two very perceptive minds, so modelling healthy communication, resolution of conflict and affection is important to me, as Bill and I live under the quiet, sometimes brooding, microscope of the teen gaze.

Of my stepfamily research dream team, Amato, Cartwright, Papernow, Bray and Hetherington, Schrodt and Nicholson, all agree that it is important for step-parents to develop positive relationships with stepchildren before attempting to take on any type of parenting role. Love first, discipline second.

'Stepparents will be more successful if they take time to get to know their children, demonstrate acceptance of them, give them support and support the parent's authority,' says Claire Cartwright. In 2009 she interviewed forty tertiary students who had experienced parents getting divorced, eighteen of whom had lived in stepfamilies when they were younger than sixteen years old. The participants' average age when they lived in a stepfamily was six years old (one that many researchers suggest makes for an easier transition for children than if they are teenagers at the time of a parent's remarriage).

Some of the quotes Cartwright included in her study, 'Relationships with Step-Parents in the Life Stories of Young Adults of Divorce' (2009), illustrate the positive impact step-parents have had on the memories and minds of their stepchildren. 'It may be desirable to focus particular clinical and research attention on assisting stepparents with an authoritarian style to adapt and cope with the demands of step parenting', Cartwright noted. The need to focus on the parenting itself, rather than who the parents are, rings true to me.

Because most of the stepfamilies with majority of time with the children have stepfathers, helping these men adjust to the new family life is a great idea. When I asked my group of friends about their childhoods and their parents' way of raising them, it was interesting that many said they had toned down or tuned up how they engaged with their kids, reacting to their own childhoods. Some who had laissez-faire parents were more involved with their kids' daily lives, and some who had strict parents were consciously less so themselves. Getting to know children before stepping into the role of disciplinarian can be quite a challenge for adults who themselves grew up with an authoritarian model of parenting.

In his article 'Living In A Stepfamily: The Child's View' (1990), Paul Amato explored what life is like in stepfamilies, and other family models, for Australian children. He interviewed 402 children living in stepfamilies, single-parent families and traditional two-parent families, half of them primary-school aged and half secondary-school aged. He talked to each for about an hour about family life, including their relationships with their parents, and rules, punishments, household chores and family activities.

The children in stepfamilies whom Amato interviewed were living in 'stepfather' stepfamilies, 'since most of our stepfamilies fell into this category'. He found that 'children in stepfamilies are not very different from other children in many respects'. For instance, there's no difference between those in stepfather families and two-parent families in their closeness to their mothers, how much help they get from their mothers, the amount of rules they make, and how often they punish them. Basically, Amato found the mother–child relationship didn't seem to be much affected by step-family life, at least from the children's point of view but 'Relations between children and stepfathers are, as you might expect, some-times problematic'.

Although most of the children Amato talked to described their stepfathers approvingly, a few were highly critical. Most of them, though, reported getting on well with their stepfathers, despite the odd disagreement: 'For example, one 9-year-old boy said, "He acts better than my ex-father. He's more intelligent and he doesn't call people names." Another 16-year-old boy said, "He's very caring, takes a close interest in everything I do and helps to see me through at school. He makes sure I get good grades."'

Amato found the longer a stepfamily had been together, the more positively the children described their relationships with their stepfathers. In stepfamilies who had been together for six years or more, the stepfather–stepchild relationship was considered to be as close as the father–child relationship in traditional families. This supports the idea that it *takes time* to build up trusting and supportive relationships within stepfamilies.

Amato also noted that stepfathers are less involved in decision-making and issuing punishments than are biological fathers in traditional families, preferring to leave the rule-making and disciplinarian roles to the children's mother. Interestingly, though, the longer children live in a stepfamily, the more likely they are to report stepfathers taking on these roles, implying that, over time, stepfathers become more like fathers in traditional families as far as stepchildren are concerned. When I asked Rupert and Gigi about this, they said they knew they were the centre of our worlds, and that we were like good cop (Bill) and bad cop (me), but both still cops!

'The quality of the child's relationship with his or her stepfather has many implications. We found that children who have positive relationships with stepfathers have high self-esteem; on the other hand, children with poor relationships with stepfathers have low self-esteem. This underscores the fact that stepfathers become central figures in children's lives—for better or for worse,' Amato says.

He also found that children in stepfamilies had more household responsibilities than do children in traditional two-parent families, which appears to carry over from their time in a single-parent household, when they needed to help out with household tasks. This equipped them with a relatively high level of everyday life skills, such as making meals, cleaning and looking after themselves. However, the children he talked to described stepfamily life as being 'somewhat less cohesive' than do children in two-parent families. They are more independent, and there is a tendency for family members to 'go their own ways' much of the time, but the longer the stepfamily has been together, the more likely members are to do things as a family.

Amato concluded that most children in Australian stepfamilies are developing well, although a small proportion of them have adjustment problems. He writes: 'Loyalty conflicts, divergent expectations, and jealousies can interfere with the development of supporting relationships in stepfamilies. Our study shows that it takes time for everyone to settle in, and for some, the amount of time involved may be frustratingly slow.'

While acknowledging that parental divorce can sometimes have negative impacts on children that carry through to their adult lives, New Zealander Penny Mansell did her PhD on the factors that caused adults to recall positive experiences of life as children in stepfamilies and their relationships with their stepmothers. She interviewed people aged between eighteen and twenty-five, all of whom as young people had lived in households with stepmothers. Some young women recalled how their stepmother had offered support that they had appreciated when needing help with 'girl issues' and with matters they felt they could not talk to their own mother about. In adulthood, some of the women came to see their stepmother as a friend, and for some who had absent mothers, the stepmother filled the mothering role over time.

We know stepmothers and stepfathers get a bad rap in the fairy-tales, and it is important we hear stories that debunk them. The stereotypes are so entrenched that Norwegian sociologist Professor Irene Levin (1997) reported 'a boy of seven insisted on telling me that she, the father's wife was NOT his stepmother, because she was not evil'. She was examining the role that gender plays in step-parenting, and analysed three different patterns of behaviour, depending on the individual's idea of family life: the 'reconstructors', the 'wait-and-see'ers' and the 'innovators'.

While not a step-parent, I suspect I started out as a 'reconstructor': one of those who have a 'notion of reconstructing a family similar to the one they had before, except that the partner is a different person'. They do not think of their new family as being of any different type or structure than the former one; for us, the nuclear family is both a model and an ideal. After several months, I realised I needed to be more like the 'wait-and-see'ers': they know that time is a 'positive resource', they progress slowly and learn as they go. They are pragmatic and don't try to emulate the nuclear family, and this type of step-parent is more a friend than parent. The innovators, Levin says, 'want to create something new and anything but the nuclear family will be acceptable'; in these families, the step-parent is more like an uncle or aunt.

Levin delved into what each model meant for couples, and how each was affected by their roles as feminine or masculine, nurturer or breadwinner, and how the couples switched between those roles. Among her findings was that the stepmother will find it harder to step back from the traditional nurturing and housekeeping role than will the stepfather. She found that couples need to eschew typical, gender-based expectations of roles within families and make their own way.

Cartwright (2014) reminds us that in the case of people who report positive and negative experiences of stepfamily life, boundary issues are often important. The parameters of the step-parent role are the most important boundary issue, as stepchildren appear to accept, and even to like, practical and emotional support from stepfathers, but disapprove of overt control or attempts to influence. They react negatively to stepfathers who make rules, impose values, control other family members, and attempt to influence or control the use of resources. Some participants in Cartwright's study reacted strongly against discipline from stepfathers, describing stepfather control as unjust or 'wrong'. On the other hand, those participants liked stepfathers who were supportive, and respected stepfathers who were careful about discipline-related boundaries.

Cartwright noted that stepfathers who engender a positive relationship, and easy and open communication, can become an integral part of stepchildren's lives and so be granted some authority. As one young woman said, 'He's got such a lovely personality that you'll do things for him, rather than because he asks you to or tells you to.' While the strongest disagreements over boundary issues were focused on control issues, participants had other ambiguous feelings. Some participants reported feeling tension between their sense that the stepfather was father-like and the knowledge that he was not (Baxter et al, 2004). Again, while others welcomed step-parental support, they rebelled against step-parental authority. Some wanted their stepfather to be like a father, and others resented their stepfather acting like a father. The message seems to be to take the cues your stepchild offers.

To sum up, it appears that step-parents who demonstrate acceptance of stepchildren, give them support, and allow the biological parent to maintain responsibility for their care and discipline, facilitate positive relationships. This is certainly something we have, slowly, learned over the years.

So, what is the best possible parenting style for non-nuclear families? As parents, there is more that unites us than divides us—trying to parent well is the aim of every parent, for all kids, in every form of family, whether single-parent, stepfamily, de facto or remarried, same-sex-parent, and so on. All children need is for their parent to believe in their ability to learn and make decisions; consistent and warm care; limit-setting guidance; other supportive adults; and the wider culture not stigmatising them if they are living in a non-nuclear family.

While Bill and I are still learning every day, I am convinced the best model is what the experts call authoritative parenting. Central to this are warmth, emotional connection, and some limit setting, so kids know and respect boundaries. I'd loved to have learned about this at school!

While I was writing about my childhood for this book, I remembered the framed poem written in 1954 that we had on the back of our bathroom door in the 1970s. I would read it over and over, and sometimes take it up with one of my parents when I felt there had been less-than-literal adherence to one credo or another. I've recently stuck the same poem to our bathroom wall, almost as a contract between us and the kids about how Bill and I will try to parent them:

Children Learn What They Live
If a child lives with criticism, he learns to condemn.
If a child lives with praise, he learns to appreciate.
If a child lives with hostility, he learns to fight.
If a child lives with tolerance, he learns to be patient.
If a child lives with ridicule, he learns to be shy.
If a child lives with encouragement, he learns confidence.
If a child lives with shame, he learns to feel guilty.
If a child lives with approval, he learns to like himself.
If a child lives with fairness, he learns justice.
If a child lives with security, he learns to have faith.
If a child lives with acceptance and friendship,
    he learns to find love in the world.

Dorothy Law Nolte PhD

This advice is so practical and yet touching in its simplicity. I'm sure our kids will take it up with us, the same way I did with my parents, if they think we're not following it strictly enough, but it's there as a reminder to all of us—stepfamily or otherwise. Even now, Clementine likes to recite parts of it to me when explaining how she feels about something. Priceless!

I knew Don Edgar (the first director of the Australian Institute of Family Studies) and Patricia Edgar (a pioneering force in quality children's television in Australia) when I was growing up, because they were friends of my parents. In their book *The New Child: In Search of Smarter Grown-Ups*, they write:

> Where a parent (in any type of family) is cold, authoritarian, and overly controlling, the child never gets to explore, they have to conform or else, so never get to know what might be possible without the fear of disapproval; they never learn to control their own behaviour or internalise the rules because control is imposed from above.
>
> On the other hand, if a parent is too permissive, simply allowing them to 'do their own thing' regardless of consequences, they get confused. Every child is testing the limits all the time, but sooner or later, in the playground or at school, they'll meet someone who won't tolerate bad, anti-social behaviour. ... In both cases—authoritarian versus permissive parenting—the child justifiably doubts that the parent gives a damn about their feelings (he hates me or he doesn't care). If there is a mix of emotional indifference plus low limit-setting, the child is left confused about what is expected, who they are and where they fit in the family scheme of things.

Jan Nicholson says:

> Many stepfamily couples struggle to find mutually acceptable parenting styles, to the detriment of children. A common pattern is for stepparents to move quickly into a disciplinary role. Often this is underpinned by beliefs that the biological parent has been too indulgent, that the children are out of control, and that they need a firm hand. Initially this role may have the implicit or explicit support of the parent. However, the consequences include children rebelling against the stepparent,

the biological parent feeling that the stepparent is too harsh or doesn't understand, and parental under-mining of the stepparent. This leads to a negatively escalating cycle, with the stepparent becoming more authoritarian, the parent becoming more permissive, increasing conflict over child rearing, and increasing child behaviour problems.

Truly 'authoritative' parenting is where there is clear emotional involvement and warmth plus limit-setting and consistent encouragement to stay within those limits. Such a combination tells the child firstly that he is a child and the parent has the power to control and keep him/her out of harm's way; secondly, that the parent loves them and is setting limits and guiding his behaviour for his own good. That parent will usually explain why, but insists that the rules be followed; they guide the child to understand gradually what is permissible, what is possible, and how to develop self-control.

In the 1960s, psychologist Diana Baumrind (1973) described three different types of parenting styles, based on her research with preschool children. Authoritative parenting, sometimes called 'democratic', involves a child–centric approach in which parents set reasonable demands and are highly responsive to their kids. While authoritative parents might have high expectations for their children, they also give their kids the resources and support they need to succeed. Baumrind said that authoritative parents: listen to their children; encourage independence; place limits, consequences, and expectations on their children's behaviour; express warmth and nurturing; allow children to express opinions and encourage them to discuss options; and administer fair and consistent discipline. I think this is a great blueprint for those times when it's unclear what the appropriate decision or response to kids' behaviour should be.

So, parents using the authoritative model want their children to learn how to reason and to work independently. If children break the rules, they are disciplined in a fair and consistent way. Such parents are also flexible; they will allow the child to explain what happened and adjust their response accordingly.

Baumrind noted that children with authoritative parents had happier dispositions, were good at managing their emotions and understanding others, developed social skills and were confident about learning new skills. Aside from consistent rules and discipline allowing children to know what to expect, authoritative parents act as role models and exhibit the same behaviour they expect from their children.

Authoritative parenting stands in contrast to the authoritarian parenting style many Australians have grown up with, characterised by exceedingly high expectations, with little warmth or guidance. (The 'Spare the rod, spoil the child method', I think it has been called.) Don Edgar points out that the family is the child's first 'teacher', and that a nurturing, supportive environment is essential for optimal development into a competent adult. Part of that teaching is to get every child to the point of having enough basic skills to operate independently in the outside world, as well as the self-belief to do so. In her book *Coping with Divorce, Single Parenting, and Remarriage*, E Mavis Hetherington found that 'authoritative parenting related to fewer behavioural problems and higher social competence whereas authoritarian parenting was associated with poorer adjustment'. Finally, Paul Amato conducted a review of father–child relationships, including stepfathers, and found authoritative parenting was more generally associated with positive psychological and social adjustment in children.

Over the decades since divorce rates spiked, following the introduction of no-fault divorce laws in Australia in the 1970s, concerns have been raised in various quarters about fathers being disparaged during times of divorce and remarriage. I know my kids' wellbeing was utterly dependent on us all having a cooperative and respectful relationship with their dad, as well as there being deep respect for Bill's role as their stepdad. There is a great deal of literature on the absence of fathers and the impact this has on their children. This complicates the discussion about the best possible support for stepfamilies because, while there have been dads who abandon their children, others have been isolated from their kids against their wishes. Reforms to family law introduced a decade ago were intended to address this, and research shows they have helped ensure kids stay linked to their fathers—which is generally a good thing all around.

The turning point in our understanding of stepfamily life came when I discovered the story of the late Emily and Dr John Visher, both step-parents, who became leading authorities on stepfamilies in the US, and would be my role-model stepfamily couple. A psychologist and psychiatrist, they spent eighteen years integrating two families that had four children in each. Having embarked on this, they found a lack of support and well-researched information, which led them to establish the Stepfamily Association of America.

From their living room in California, the Vishers started the first modern stepfamily organisation, to help themselves and others learn how to make stepfamilies work as well as they possibly can. Their first members' conference was held in December 1979 and attracted media attention, after which they were inundated with calls from stepfamilies wanting to be part of a larger group of people who were living just like they were. The Vishers reported, 'people were so happy to have someone to talk with who understood where they were coming from'. They also noted: 'Stepfamilies are also often viewed through a nuclear family lens. Unfortunately, this use of a nuclear family frame can maintain unhelpful step-family myths, privilege the biological parent role, and stigmatise the stepparent roles' (Visher, 1979).

The Stepfamily Association of America has since become an important resource for families all over the world, as well as those wanting to give their clients, students, listeners, viewers or readers quality information. Its primary emphasis is on research-based stepfamily information for families and the media, and it has explored stepfamily strengths and tribulations across North America, South America, Europe, Asia, Africa, Australia and New Zealand. Demand for the association's services grew so large that its volunteer staff struggled to cope, which, in part, was the impetus for the founding of the National Stepfamily Resource Center in 2006, as part of Auburn University's Center for Children, Youth, and Families. Wouldn't it be wonderful if we had that kind of invest-ment of resources in what is 43 per cent of Australia's families?

The Vishers had a vision that stepfamilies would one day be accepted, supported and successful. The cumulative result of their work was creating a turning point for all of us who live and love in stepfamilies. Through their research, writing, and speaking, John and Emily Visher showed that living in a stepfamily is a truly remarkable opportunity to have a diverse and fulfilling family experience. We owe them a debt, individually and as a society, as different family styles continue to proliferate.

Despite the positive work of people like the Vishers, parents in non-nuclear families continue to be let down by assumptions we don't have the same chance as other parents of producing happy and solid families. This is despite all the findings that there are other reasons than simply being part of a stepfamily why children may not thrive, such as the conflict they were exposed to before their parent's remarriage. Finding out the extent, or not, to which stepfamily life is actually the source of any problems requires further study. As Chandler Arnold says, in *Children and Stepfamilies: A Snapshot*, 'When we read the worrying impacts of family breakup and stepfamily problems we don't necessarily understand that many of the behavior problems associated with children raised in step-families are likely caused by pre-existing conflicts experienced by these children, not by the fact that they are raised by a stepparent.'

It would be hugely encouraging were the research into, and public discussion about, stepfamilies to highlight at least some of the positive experiences that they and other non-nuclear families have, while remaining aware of the challenges. It needs to be recognised that there are prospering, joyful non-nuclear families, where children are demonstrably better off than if they were living in an abusive, neglectful or otherise unloving home. Arnold comments that 'Researchers are often guilty of ... for example, repeatedly compar[ing] the self-esteem or problems of children in step-families with children in other family types instead of attempting to pinpoint the factors contributing to positive self-esteem in other stepfamily children.'

He also points out 'there is no evidence that behavior identi-fied as optimal functioning in nuclear families is the same behavior seen as optimal functioning in stepfamilies, and repeated attempts to highlight these apparent differences may obscure possible func-tional alternatives possible in step relationships'. In other words, we must allow stepfamilies to have their own identities and models, and not constantly compare them with nuclear-family models. I don't compare my children's relationship with their dad to the one they have with their stepdad; each of them is special in its own way. What matters is the wellbeing of the children.

We need to ensure professionals in the field of family research are aware of their own prejudices, and have expertise in stepfamily and other family foundations, rather than predicating their work on rigid nuclear-family models. Our communities, and institutions, including schools and churches, should rally around new families, and provide an optimistic and supportive environment, particularly in the family's early stages. While many people would, no doubt, be ready to do this, they may not realise how much difference their support can make.

And people need to be willing to put aside myths, which individuals can internalise, affecting their view of themselves and becoming impediments to them functioning healthily. I dearly wish I'd found the below list eight years ago. I would not be at all surprised if the following myths, all of which need debunking, had application to non-nuclear families too.

The National Stepfamily Resource Center busts the following myths that influence people's views about stepfamilies:

Myth #1—Love occurs instantly between the child and the stepparent
This is the expectation that because you love your new partner you will automatically love his or her children; or that the children will automatically love us because we are such nice people. Of course, if we think about it, we recognize that establishing relationships takes time; that it does not happen overnight or by magic.

Even if we recognize the time involved, it is hard to accept that sometimes we are willing to have a relationship with someone who is not willing to have a relationship with us. That hurts, and when people hurt, they may become resentful and angry.

Stepfamily adjustment will be helped if we come to the relationships with our stepchildren with minimal, and, therefore, more realistic, expectations about how the relationships will develop. We may then be pleased when respect and friendship blossom and less disappointed if it takes more time than we anticipated.

Myth #2—Children of divorce and remarriage are forever damaged

Children go through a painful period of adjustment after a divorce or remarriage. Adults often respond to their children's pain with guilt. Somehow they feel they can 'make it up' to them. This leads to difficulties in responding appropriately to our children's hurt and setting appropriate limits—an important part of parenting.

Researchers have hopeful news about children of divorce and remarriage. Although it takes some time, most children do recover their emotional equilibrium. Five and 10 years later most are found to be no different, in many important ways, from kids in first marriage families.

Myth #3—Stepmothers are wicked

This myth is based on the fairy stories we all hear as children. Because these stories tell about stepmothers who are not kind, nice or fair, we may be confused about our roles when we become stepmothers. We are nice people, wanting to do a good job, but the world seems to have another idea about stepmothers.

This negative concept of the stepmother role impacts us in a very personal way and we may be very self-conscious about our step-parenting. Research tells us that stepmothers have the most difficult role in the stepfamily. (But, if you are a stepmother, you knew that already!)

Myth #4—Adjustment to stepfamily life occurs quickly
People are optimistic and hopeful when they remarry. They want life to settle down and to get on with being happy. If your hope or expectation is that once the wedding vows are spoken life will return to normal (whatever that is), you are going to be disappointed.

Because stepfamilies are such complicated families, the time it takes for people to get to know each other, to create positive relationships, and to develop some family history is significant, usually at least four years.

Myth #5—Children adjust to divorce and remarriage more easily if biological fathers (or mothers) withdraw
Children will always have two biological parents, and will adjust better if they can access both. This means they need to be able to see their nonresidential parent and to think well of him or her. Sometimes visitation is painful for the nonresidential parent, but it is very important to the child's adjustment and emotional health, except in those rare instances of parental abuse or neglect.

It helps if the residential parent and stepparent can work toward a 'parenting partnership' with all the adults involved. Sometimes this can't happen right away, but it can be something to work toward.

Myth #6—Stepfamilies formed after a parent dies are easier
People need time to grieve the loss of a loved one, and a remarriage may 'reactivate' unfinished grieving. These emotional issues may get played out in the new relationship with detrimental effects.

Another problem is that it can be difficult to think realistically about the person who has died. He or she exists in memory, not in reality, and sometimes gets elevated to sainthood.

When people remarry after the death of a spouse, they may want a relationship similar to the one before. When people remarry after a divorce, they are usually looking for something very different. New partners may find themselves competing with a ghost.

Myth #7—Part-time stepfamilies are easier
Relationships take time. Stepfamilies where the children only visit occasionally are hampered by the lack of time to work on relationships.

If your stepchildren come every other weekend, there is less time for one-on-one time between the stepchild and stepparent, and less time for family activities. Since stepfamilies follow an adjustment process (stages of development), it may take the part-time stepfamily longer to move through the process.

Myth #8—There is only one kind of family
This is the myth that says you will be just like a first marriage (or biological) family. Today there are lots of different kinds of families; first marriage, single parent, foster, and stepfamilies to name a few. Each is valuable and has different characteristics. Just because there are two adults in the stepfamily doesn't mean that it recreates a biological family. If this is what you are hoping for, you will be frustrated when it doesn't happen.

All new parents, of course, deserve high-quality information; it still amazes me that parenting practices aren't in the curriculum of ante-natal classes. The responsibility and pressure placed on a new step-parent can be a shock to the system. To assist in preventing unhelpful patterns of interaction and habits starting, stepfamilies need access to the best, and detailed, advice.

I've spent time on a mental-health foundation board in Queensland. I've been involved in the promotion of psychological and emotional wellbeing in the workplace, and worked on fundraising for youth suicide prevention. So it won't surprise anyone to hear that I am a big advocate of expert advice and getting the best possible information. I don't think seeking this out is an admission of failure; it's the reverse.

If I were doing it all again from scratch, starting our stepfamily again from the ground up, I would try to connect with other new stepfamilies through organisations like Stepfamilies Australia or Relationships Australia; even an online group of parents in similar situations would have been helpful. Because, as we've seen, so much of the professional help for non-nuclear families is based on what's called a deficit comparison, the data the counsellors and therapists have to work from is often from the point of view that something needs fixing, rather than that it is new and needs incubating. But people don't want to feel as though seeking help is an admission of failure.

Find practitioners who have expertise in family therapy or counselling stepfamilies, says Monash University psychologist Dr Cate Bearsley-Smith. She points out that family therapy models are usually based on nuclear families, and often don't meet the unique, and sometimes complex, needs of stepfamilies. Dr Bearsley-Smith calls on clinicians to develop expertise that can address the alliances that exist within families of origin at the family's formation; and also any unresolved issues, such as uncertainty about and conflict regarding new family norms, boundaries, and the unique environmental (such as legal, financial, logistical and social) pressures.

I found when I sought advice from a specialist who wasn't specifically trained in stepfamilies that, while they had our best interests at heart, the examples they provided were too one-size-fits-all, and their knowledge of some of the external pressures due to divorce and repartnering was plainly incorrect. When therapists are 'equipped with an understanding of the pressures that step-families face', they can 'more effectively target interventions', in the words of Bearsley-Smith.

'Intervention' is the official term for the methods of counselling and teaching that help each member of a family define rules, roles, boundaries and to build the shared experiences that make a family—of any structure—connect. An effective clinician will understand the specific challenges of stepfamily and non-nuclear-family life, and also understand myths such as that of 'instant love'. Unpacking the different parts of the family suitcase, the clinician can help each member know what their role is, and give them the tools to construct a household that suits them all. As well, help in dealing with the grief or worry resulting from divorce is liberating for the family members.

When you feel you are not wholly responsible for everyone else's response, and you don't have to compare yourself to the nuclear families around you, it is a relief and allows you to get on with the job of creating your family. As the Australian Psychological Society says, the specialists' purpose is 'to clearly map the family structure, roles and functional boundaries'. Fragile sub-systems, such as the new couple at the centre of the family, need to be strengthened, while other coalitions may need to change. The building of shared experiences, should be encouraged and competing developmental needs respected.

The AIFS lays out the groundwork for non-nuclear families, and I'd have loved my marriage certificate to have come with a copy of their *Family Matters* newsletter. Then there is Jan Nicholson, another 'Professor of Families', as I like to call them, with a substantial body of work dedicated to families, parenting and public health; she heads the Transition to Contemporary Parenthood Program at Monash University. When I read her work, I thought, 'I'm signing up now!'

I certainly don't regret using programs to help us transition to being a stepfamily, and I often feel like we all need a 'step coach'. And doing all the reading I needed to do to write this book has led to a series of lightbulb moments.

10

It takes a village
to raise a family

WHEN I WAS a new mother for the first time, I was all at sea
for a while. There was the wonderful love I felt, and then
there were all the expectations of what it means to be a mother,
and of how it 'should' be done. It was a time of learning, hoping,
advice from the sidelines, and anxious, sleepless nights. I questioned
myself and my abilities, and was trying so hard to do everything
the correct way, the best way, that it could get overwhelming.
Sometimes, I would get so exasperated with the conflicting advice
that new mothers are bombarded with from multiple sources, I'd
want to throw all the baby books in the bin. Yet, although the
sudden transition from non-mother to mother made me feel
vulnerable at times, I could sense the community's support.

When I took my baby boy out in the pram, there would be coos
of admiration and good wishes all around. Every new mum will tell
you how free people feel to share the beauty of a new baby with

the proud parent, even if they're a stranger, and having someone reach out warmly to you in this way is a small, but important, sign that you have support. There were helpful nurses, magazines with articles about being a new parent were readily available and friends bought meals. The local maternal health clinic coordinated parents' groups, and the church had groups for parents. It felt like there was an expectation in the community that new families are looked out for.

When I remarried and was having my third child, there was something of the same feeling, but I reflect on how things would have been had the fledgling stepfamily had a similar scaffold around its warm, but unfamiliar, new nest. After I moved to Melbourne, I never felt like I was starting from scratch as a parent, but I was concerned about the older children, and how to help them cope with their feelings of loss and change. It felt like a new voyage, one taken without a compass or a map.

I went about making my new family following my instincts from my previous experience with marriage and family, and nurtured my precious new baby as best I could. This helped me up to a point: that is, until I started questioning those instincts and realised I needed more information. Without models of the kind we have all around us of nuclear families in various stages of development, I thought I had perhaps thrown myself into the task with a misplaced sense of complacency, and that there were so many elements to think about that my mothering skills weren't sufficient. I felt guilty because I didn't think I would be able necessarily to handle every situation in the stepfamily-building process as deftly as I had in my first two kids' early childhoods. I also perceived that the environment around new stepfamilies is not as implicitly supportive and validating—and optimistic—as it is around brand-new nuclear families.

It is hard to articulate something unsaid but I've noticed the different attitude that exists towards the creation of a stepfamily and the creation of a nuclear family with the arrival of a baby, even though they are both worth celebrating. Parents I've spoken to have told me that a reassuring hand, and some understanding from those around them that they're in uncharted, emotional and exciting territory, would be most welcome. Just as it always is when you bring home your new baby.

I strongly believe that if we blew away the clouds of stigma and stereotypes, families like mine would be much more likely to pleasantly surprise the community, and less likely to suffer the fate of some stepfamilies and come apart within the first few years. Jan Nicholson, 'Professor of Families', told me: 'Remarried couples can have quite a hard time when they get together. They can face criticism from family and friends, and their new relationship may spark renewed conflict with an ex-spouse. For those whose relationship started as an affair when one or both were still married, they may face considerable hostility from people around them. In this atmosphere, it is natural to put on a united "happy" front, to prove to the world that you have done the right thing.

'Many couples will let things slide, pretend that they are coping and avoid seeking help for minor problems, which then escalate over time and become established patterns'. She points out that 'by the time stepfamily couples seek help, their problems can be really quite severe and entrenched.'

So, starting early, and with a preventive focus, is important. We need to normalise seeking information and support, so that people in any type of family, but especially stepfamilies and other non-nuclear families, are empowered to obtain the resources to help them build a positive future together and handle the inevitable cascade of challenges that family brings.

There are so many people starting stepfamilies who are resource-poor and doing everything they can to ensure their family is healthy, yet struggle for support. To let them languish with a sense of not being as welcome in the 'family' tent as every other family is inherently wrong. New mothers and fathers need goodwill, as do new stepmothers and stepfathers; they shouldn't need to appear 'broken' in order to receive support. For instance, a dedicated online support service for stepfamilies or other non-nuclear families would be a marvellous step in this direction. Groups along the lines of council-organised mothers' groups but for parents forming new stepfamilies or other non-nuclear families, and open to peer support (both receiving and offering it), could also be a huge help.

Coming into contact with the bias that stepfamilies are less worthy of affirmation than nuclear families makes me sigh, because it seems mired in a set of prejudices that deny reality. Those who argue for the supremacy of nuclear families over others, based on their narrow definition of what is a real family, may damage perceptions of other families and aren't exactly loving thy neighbour. A lot of the issues that come up in arguments about which family type is 'ideal' for children are overly focused on the form of the family, not on how effectively it functions; this is a very superficial way to weigh up what works for individual children and families. And talking stepfamilies down is self-defeating for the whole community, especially when you consider that the health and wellbeing of families generally is crucial to the health and wellbeing of the whole nation, including the economy and the workforce.

Professor Alan Hayes, former director of the AIFS for over a decade, is now foundation chair of family studies at the University of Newcastle. He says, 'Diversity and change have always characterised families, and increasingly do so. The functions families fulfil are perennial, and the key concern is how societies and communities support families to function well and minimise the negative impacts of outdated stereotypes.'

Quite apart from having educated myself about the data and statistics on, and latest academic understanding of, stepfamilies, I have learned a lot about myself, and real-world parenting, in the last eight years. I would advise other people taking the trip into unknown family territory not to be too hard on themselves, as I've had to learn not to be too hard on myself. (There is such a concept, as the late pediatrician and psychiatrist Donald Winnicott put it, of 'the ordinary, good enough parent', who has 'the sound instincts of normal parents, stable and healthy families'.)

Never underestimate the strength and resilience of your family, and especially of the children, and their capacity to be compassionate, broad-minded and generally decent. Parenting is amazingly rewarding but difficult in a vacuum, and I've had to learn on the go about this new family style. The good news is that, having made it this far, I am finally more confident and have discovered reserves of courage I didn't know I had. My belief is that other people who are able to hang in there, and keep putting one foot after the other in building their stepfamily, will also surprise themselves.

Again, stepfamilies have been with us through the ages. In ancient Greece and Rome, remarriage following death or divorce ensured that stepfamilies were relatively common. From the 1530s, the Catholic Church begin detailed record keeping about all the European nobles, including their stepfamilies. However, even when a large part of the population are stepfamilies or other non-nuclear families, with other generations living in the same household, practices and policies are still focused on nuclear families. This has left us with a narrow view of what a healthy, happy family is.

By 2050 families will be even more diverse, and all of them should expect understanding and support.

I'm not a clinician, academic or practitioner, I'm a mother, and I've started to realise that itself is enough expertise to make a stepfamily work. I would describe establishing a stepfamily, while going through the usual milestones and passages in life, as wheels within wheels. I know that making sure all those moving parts are healthy and not squeaky is unrelenting for parents; you just have to keep turning up and spraying on the metaphorical RP7.

I've been asked how you know as a step-parent when you're 'in the groove' and can know you've made it into calm waters. While having learned not to be over-vigilant or under-strict to compensate my children for the path I chose for them, I have also learned to keep an eye out for the signs that everything is going well and is as it should be. I believe in the saying 'You're only as happy as your unhappiest child', and my experience is that when your children are happy and well, you're in that zone too.

Any family has stages when you're all going along nicely and then one child takes a tumble and you have to focus on that. You know intrinsically when your child is okay or not okay. In my experience, signs they're okay include that they're happy to go to school, have friends, and are talking to you; these are simple little things but telling. Your children don't have to be highly successful in any particular field of endeavour, just settled. But don't let yourself get trapped into looking for problems when there is a very good chance that, given your instinct isn't screaming at you that something's not right, no problem exists. Trust yourself.

To the next mother starting out building a stepfamily, I'd say this: you will amaze yourself. When you feel like you've had a setback or failure, remember it's part of making progress. You're not supposed to know how to do it all straightaway, just like when you come home with a first baby, or start a new job; it's all right to be rubbish at times, it will pass. You'll constantly encounter things you didn't know about before, because nobody gave you a handbook. It's important to reach out to others, and I think it's a shame if we have to try to summon up courage to reach out. That's really what I want to see changed: that people in new stepfamilies don't have to reach out; that people reach out to them, as they do to anyone with having their first baby. Friendships formed in parenting groups are often crucial, making the difference between things being okay or being pretty ordinary, and that network needs to exist for new stepfamilies.

To men who are joining an existing family unit and haven't yet had children of their own, as was Bill's situation, I'd say that the process of everyone adjusting is not quick and easy, like making a packet cake! Take the pressure off yourself, and just be friends with the children for a long while; take it slow. Remember that stepfathers are special and can make a huge difference to someone's life. As my dad says, love their mother; that's the best thing you can do for them.

To kids getting a new stepfather or stepmother, I'd say don't feel that you need to bond instantly with this new person in your life; get to know each other. It takes lots of talking, and you have the right to be heard. Lots of families are stepfamilies and things with them are fine; you have more people to love you now, but it will take a while to adjust and not feel so much hurt. You will adjust, though, as time goes by.

During my research, I asked Paul Amato what he would say to a step-parent if they were doubting themselves. His answer rang true: 'Members of stepfamilies (compared with families with two biological parents) sometimes have to work a little harder to make everything work well. But most members eventually figure out how to do this pretty well—sometimes with a little counselling, and sometimes on their own. When family life gets difficult, they should remember that all families face challenges and go through hard times. No one ever said that family life is stress free.'

What I have learned from my reading for this book is that families, regardless of their structures, are more similar than they are different. Family members want to be loved and loving, cared for, included, and valued for who they are, not what kind of family they belong to. I hope this book enlightens people who are not in stepfamilies about their upsides, and shows that they need understanding, especially at first, when they are going into uncharted waters, optimistically but sometimes feeling quite alone. I hope I've helped to challenge the stereotypes, and demonstrated that having a disapproving, or otherwise negative, attitude to stepfamilies and other non-nuclear families is potentially quite harmful, and has to change.

The long-term research has taught us a lot about stepfamilies, and that they have a high rate of success in raising healthy children. At least 80 per cent of the kids in stepfamilies do fine, but that is not a statistic we hear much. What hurts stepchildren has little to do with stepfamilies per se; it is much more likely to be parental conflict left over from the first marriage. While expectations about women's roles and responsibilities can cause problems in stepfamilies, many stepfamilies after the first five years are more stable than many first-marriage families, having experienced most of their troubles in the first two years. So, my message is to hang in there.

We've learned that members of stepfamilies experience real gains: notably, the opportunity to thrive due to there being a happier couple relationship. We know that stepkids are resilient, and that understanding what makes them so will help all Australian families.

Families are highly diverse in their formations but it's the way they function that is important. Although divorce and remarriage confront families with stresses and adaptive challenges, they also offer opportunities for personal growth, and more fulfilling family and other personal relationships. Of course, I am not pro-divorce; you could describe me as pro-marriage but all for dealing with realities. Social norms have shifted, family types have diversified, and people have become more tolerant, though it would be wonderful if they were even more so.

When I told my family I wanted to write about non-nuclear families, and specifically about our own family, they were a little hesitant—and I don't blame them. I put my case by saying, 'There are some things we've learned in the past eight years that are so simple I'd like to tell other stepfamilies about them, so they can start off with confidence and a little less drama.' Although they thought my reasons for telling our story were good ones, they were concerned about privacy. However, sometimes a more sensitive public discourse reveals that we all have more in common with each other than we have pushing us apart. So, my family and I decided together that because stepfamilies matter and might be able to use some help, especially the vulnerable ones, we should go ahead with sharing our story.

I believe passionately that we need more voices in the national conversation, including those of stepfamilies, sole-parent families, grandparent-raised families, same-sex-parent families and adoptive families. My vision is for us all to take, as my mentor and friend Wendy McCarthy puts it, 'the long view', to help all Australia's families be optimistic, resilient and flourishing.

Bibliography

Allan, G, Crow, G and Hawker, S (2011), *Stepfamilies*, London: Palgrave, Macmillan

AM (2014), 'Children raised by same-sex couples happier and healthier, research suggests', ABC News Radio

Amato, P (1994), 'Father–child relations, mother–child relations and offspring psychological wellbeing in early adulthood', *Journal of Marriage and Family*, vol 56, no 4, pp 1031–42

Amato, P (1993), 'Children's adjustment to divorce: Theories, hypotheses and empirical support', *Journal of Marriage and Family*, vol 55, no 1, pp 23–8

Amato, P (1990), 'Living in a stepfamily: The child's view', *Stepfamilies*, www.stepfamilies.info (National Stepfamily Resource Center)

Amato, P and Cheadle, J (2005), 'The long reach of divorce: Divorce and child well-being across three generations', *Journal of Marriage and Family*, vol 67, no 1, pp 191–206

Amato, P, King, V and Thorsen, M L (2016), 'Parent–child relationships in stepfather families and adolescent adjustment: A latent class analysis', *Journal of Marriage and Family*, vol 78, no 2, pp 482–97

Amato, P and Sobolewski, J M, 'The effects of divorce and marital discord on adult children's psychological well-being', *American Sociological Review*, vol 66, no 6, pp 900–21

Appleton, S F (2013), 'Family laws equality project in our empirical age' in McClain, L and Cere, D (eds), *What is Parenthood: Contemporary Debates about the Family*, New York: NYU Press

Arnold, C (1998), 'Children and stepfamilies: A snapshot', *Centre for Law and Social Policy*, www.clasp.org

Atwood, J D (1990), '10 necessary steps to stepfamily integration', *Marriage and Family Living*, pp 20–5, Hoboken: Wiley-Blackwell

Attar-Schwartz, S et al (2009), 'Grandparenting and adolescent adjustment in two-parent biological, lone-parent and step-parent families', *Journal of Family Psychology*, vol 23, no 1, pp 67–75

Australian Bureau of Statistics (2012–13), *Reflecting a Nation: Stories from the 2011 Census*, 'Same-sex couple families', Canberra: Australian Government

Australian Institute of Family Studies (2016), *Growing Up in Australia: The Longitudinal Study of Australian Children Annual Statistical Report 2015*, Canberra: Australian Government

Australian Institute of Family Studies (2007), *Stepfamilies: Understanding and Responding Effectively*, Melbourne: Australian Government

Australian Institute of Health and Welfare (2012), *A Picture of Australia's Children 2012*, cat no PHE 167, Canberra: AIHW

Baumrind, D (1973), 'The development of instrumental competence through socialization', in Pick, A (ed), *Minnesota Symposia on Child Psychology*, vol 7, pp 3–46

Baxter, J (2016a), *Diversity, Complexity and Change in Children's Households*, Melbourne: Australian Institute of Family Studies

Baxter, J (2016b), 'The modern Australian family' (Facts Sheet), Melbourne: Australian Institute of Family Studies

Baxter, J (2015) in Australian Institute of Family Studies, *Longitudinal Study of Australian Children*, LSAC Annual Statistical Report, ch 3, 'Diversity, complexity and change in children's households', Melbourne: AIFS

Baxter, L, Braithwaite, D, Bryant, L and Wagner, A (2004), 'Stepchildren's perceptions of the contradictions in communications with stepparents', *Journal of Social and Personal Relationships*, vol 21, pp 447–67

Baxter, L, Braithwaite, D and Nicholson, J (1999), 'Turning points in the development of blended families', *Journal of Social and Personal Relationships*, vol 16, p 291

Bearsley-Smith, C (2007), 'Adapting family therapy for stepfamilies', *InPsych*, 2007, article 5

Bengtson, V L (2001), 'Beyond the nuclear family: The increasing importance of multigenerational bonds', *Journal of Marriage and Family*, vol 63, no 1, pp 1–16

Biblarz, T and Savci, E (2010), 'Lesbian, gay, bisexual and transgender families', *Journal of Marriage and Family*, vol 72, no 3, pp 480–97

Bowes, J, Grace, R and Hodge, K (2012), *Children, Families and Communities: Contexts and Consequences*, South Melbourne: Oxford University Press

Bray, J and Kelly, J (1999), *Stepfamilies: Love, Marriage, and Parenting in the First Decade*, New York: Broadway

Bray, J and Berger, S H (1990), 'Non-custodial parent and grandparent relationships in stepfamilies', *Family Relations*, vol 39, pp 414–19

Bray, J and Hetherington, E M (1993), 'Families in transition: Introduction and overview', *Journal of Family Psychology*, vol 7, no 1, pp 3–8

Bryce, Q (2013), *Boyer Lectures 2013*, 'Back to Grassroots', Sydney: Harper Collins

Cahn, N (2013), *The New Kinship: Constructing Donor Conceived Families*, New York: NYU Press

Cartwright, C (2014), 'Step-parenting', in *Families, Policy and the Law*, pp 101–5, Melbourne: Australian Institute of Family Studies

Cartwright, C (2012), 'The challenges of being a mother in a stepfamily', *Journal of Divorce and Remarriage*, vol 53, no 6, pp 503–11

Cartwright, C (2010), 'Preparing to re-partner and live in a stepfamily: An exploratory investigation', *Journal of Family Studies*, vol 16, no 3, pp 237–50

Cartwright, C (2006), 'You want to know how it affected me? Young adults' perceptions of the impact of parental divorce', *Journal of Divorce and Remarriage*, vol 44, nos 3–4, pp 125–43

Cartwright, C (2005), 'Stepfamily living and parent–child relationships: An exploratory investigation', *Journal of Family Studies*, vol 11, no 2, pp 267–83

Cartwright, C, Farnsworth, V and Mobley, V (2009), 'Relationships with step-parents in the life stories of young adults of divorce', *Family Matters*, vol 82, June 2009, p 30

Cartwright, C and Gibson, K (2013), 'The effects of co-parenting relationships with ex-spouses on couples and step-families', *Family Matters*, vol 92, pp 18–28

Cartwright, C and Seymour, F (2002) 'Young adults' perceptions of parents' responses in stepfamilies. What hurts? What helps?' *Journal of Divorce and Remarriage*, vol 37, pp 123–41

Cassells, R, Toohey, M, Keegan, M and Mohanty, I (2013), *Modern Family: The Changing Shape of Australian Families*, Report of the National Centre for Social and Economic Modelling, Bruce: University of Canberra

Cherlin, A (1978), 'Remarriage as an incomplete institution', *American Journal of Sociology*, vol 84, no 3, pp 634–50

Clinton, H (1996), *It Takes a Village: And Other Lessons Children Teach Us*, New York: Simon & Schuster

Coleman, M, Fine, M A, Ganong, L H, Downs, K J M and Pauk, N (2001), 'When you're not the Brady Bunch: Identifying perceived conflicts and resolution strategies in stepfamilies', *Personal Relationships*, vol 8, no 1, pp 55–73

Coleman, M, Ganong, L and Fine, M (2000), 'Reinvestigating remarriage: Another decade of progress', *Journal of Marriage and Family*, vol 62, no 4, pp 1288–1307

Coleman, M, Ganong, L and Gingrich, R (1985), 'Stepfamily strengths: A review of popular literature', *Journal of Family Relations*, vol 34, no 4, pp 583–9

Coleman, M, Ganong, L and Goodwin, C (1994), 'The presentation of stepfamilies in marriage and family textbooks: A re-examination', *Family Relations*, vol 43, no 3, pp 289–97

Crosbie-Burnett, M (1984), 'The centrality of the step relationship: A challenge to family theory and practice', *Family Relations*, vol 33, pp 459–63

Crosbie-Burnett, M and Giles-Sims, J (1994), 'Adolescent adjustment and step-parenting styles', *Family Relations*, vol 43, no 4, pp 394–9

De Vaus, D (2004), *Diversity and Change in Australian Families*, Melbourne: Australian Institute of Family Studies

Edgar, P and Edgar, D (2008), *The New Child: In Search of Smarter Grown-ups*, Melbourne: Wilkinson Publishing

Edwards, J N, 'New conceptions: Biosocial innovations and the family', *Journal of Marriage and Family*, vol 53, no 2, pp 349–60

Feeney, J A and Planitz, J M (2009), 'Are step-siblings bad, stepmothers wicked, and stepfathers evil? An assessment of Australian stepfamily stereotypes', *Journal of Family Studies*, vol 15, no 1, pp 82–97

Feinberg, M K, Kan, M L and Hetherington, M E (2007), 'The longitudinal influence of co-parenting conflict on parental negativity and adolescent maladjustment', *Journal of Marriage and Family*, vol 69, no 3, pp 687–702

Finch, J (1989), *Family Obligations and Social Change*, Cambridge: Polity Press

Fine, M A and Kurdek, L A (1995), 'Relations between marital quality and step-parent child relationship quality for parents and stepparents in stepfamilies', *Journal of Family Psychology*, vol 9, no 2, pp 216–23

Francis, L and Millear, P (2015), 'Mastery or misery: Conflict between separated parents a psychological burden for children', *Journal of Divorce and Remarriage*, vol 56, no 7, pp 551–68

Freisthler, B, Messick Svare, G S and Harrison-Jay, S (2008), 'It was the best of times, it was the worst of times: Young adult stepchildren talk about growing up in a stepfamily', *Journal of Divorce and Remarriage*, vol 38, September 2008, pp 83–102

Ganong, L and Coleman, M (2016), *Stepfamily Relationships: Development, Dynamics, and Interventions*, New York: Springer Science+Business Media

Ganong, L and Coleman, M (1997), 'How society views stepfamilies', *Marriage and Family Review*, vol 26, 85–106

Ganong, L, Coleman, M, Fine, M and Martin, P (1999), 'Stepparents' affinity-seeking and affinity-maintaining strategies with stepchildren', *Journal of Family Issues*, vol 20, pp 299–327

Glick, P (1988), 'Fifty years of family demography: A record of social change', *Journal of Marriage and Family*, vol 50, no 4

Glick, P and Gold, J (2015), 'Intergenerational attachments in stepfamilies', *The Family Journal: Counseling and Therapy for Couples and Families*, vol 32, no 2, pp 194–200

Golish, T (2003), 'Stepfamily communication strengths: Understanding the ties that bind', *Human Communication Research*, vol 29, no 1, pp 41–80

Gorrell Barnes, G, Thompson, P, Daniel, G and Burkhardt, N (1998), *Growing Up in Stepfamilies*, Oxford: Clarendon Press

Greenspan, L M and Deardorff, J (2014), *The New Puberty*, Emmaus: Rodale, Inc

Hayes, A (2016), interview with the author

Hayes, A (2015), 'Building stronger Australians', paper presented at the Building Australian Families Forum, Canberra

Hayes, A and Higgins, D (2014), *Families, Policy and the Law: Selected Essays on Contemporary Issues for Australia*, Melbourne: Australian Institute of Family Studies

Hayes, A, Weston, R and Qu, L (2010), *Families Then and Now: 1980–2010*, Melbourne: Australian Institute of Family Studies

Hetherington, E M (2014), 'Coping with divorce, single parenting, and remarriage: A risk and resiliency perspective', *Single Parenting*, 19 March 2013

Hetherington, E M (1999), 'The adjustment of children with divorced parents: A risk and resiliency perspective', *Journal of Child Psychology and Psychiatry*, vol 40, no 1, pp 129–40

Hetherington, E M (1993), 'An overview of the Virginia Longitudinal Study of Divorce and Remarriage with a focus on early adolescence', *Journal of Family Psychology*, vol 7, no 1, pp 39–56

Hetherington, E M and Kelly, J (2002), *For Better or For Worse: Divorce Reconsidered*, New York: Norton

Jones, A C (2003), 'Reconstructing the stepfamily: Old myths, new stories', *Social Work*, vol 48, no 2

Ju Shin, Y, Kyu Lee, J and Miller-Day, M (2013), 'The effects of maternal emotional wellbeing on mother–adolescent communication and youth emotional wellbeing', *Communication Research Reports*, vol 30, no 2, pp 137–47

Kelley, D L and Sequeira, D L (1997), 'Understanding family functioning in a changing America', *Communication Studies*, vol 48, pp 93–107

Kaspiew, R, Gray, M, Weston, R, Moloney, L, Hand, K and Qu, L (2009), 'Evaluation of the 2006 family law reforms', Report, Australian Institute of Family Studies, Melbourne

Kinniburgh-White, R, Cartwright, C and Seymour, F (2010), 'Young adults' narratives of relational development with step-fathers', *Journal of Social and Personal Relationships*, vol 27, no 7, pp 890–907

Kovacs, G T, Wise, S and Finch, S (2013), 'Functioning of families with primary school age children conceived using anonymous donor sperm', *Human Reproduction*, vol 28, no 2, pp 375–84

Lawton, J M and Sanders, M R (1994), 'Designing effective behavioral family interventions for stepfamilies', *Clinical Psychology Review*, vol 14, pp 463–96

Leon, K and Angst, E (2005), 'Portrayals of stepfamilies in film: Using media images in remarriage education', *Family Relations*, vol 54, no 1, pp 3–23

Levin, I (1997), 'The stepparent role from a gender perspective', *Marriage and Family Review*, vol 26, nos 1–2, pp 177–90

Lucas, N, Erbas, B and Nicholson, J M (2013), 'Child mental health after parental separation: The impact of resident/non-resident parenting, parent mental health, conflict and socioeconomics', *Journal of Family Studies*, vol 19, no 1, pp 53–69

McClain, L and Cere, D (2013), 'A diversity approach to parenthood in family life and family law' in McClain, L and Cere, D (eds), *What is Parenthood? Contemporary Debates about the Family*, pp 41–57, New York: NYU Press

McDonald, P (1992), 'Extended family in Australia: The family beyond the household', *Family Matters*, vol 32, pp 1–10

Mackay, R (2003), 'Family resilience and good child outcomes: An overview of the research literature', *Social Policy Journal of New Zealand*, issue 20

Magnuson, K B and Berger, L M (2009), 'Family structure states and transitions: Associations with children's wellbeing during middle childhood', *Journal of Marriage and Family*, vol 71, no 3, pp 575–91

Mansell, P (2011), 'Young adult stepchildren's experiences of relationship with stepmothers', (PhD thesis, Doctor of Clinical Psychology), University of Auckland

Maynes, M J and Waltner, A (2012), *The Family: A World History*, New York: Oxford University Press

Mental Health Social Support (2012), '*Trends and Statistics of the Contemporary Family*', retrieved from http://www.aipc.net.au/articles/trends-and-statistics-of-the-contemporary-family/

Meredith, L, Sherbourne, C, Gaillot, S, Hansell, L, Ritschard, H V, Parker, A M and Wrenn, G (2011), *Promoting Psychological Resilience in the US Military*, Santa Monica: RAND Corporation

Metts, S, Braithwaite, D, Schrodt, P, Wang, T, Holman, A, Nuru, A and Abetz, J S (2013), 'The experience and expression of stepchildren's emotions at critical events in stepfamily life', *Journal of Divorce and Remarriage*, vol 54, no 5

Minuchin, S and Fishman, H C (1981, revised in 2009), *Family Therapy Techniques*, Cambridge, Massachusetts: Harvard University Press

Montgomery, J and Fewer, M I (1988), *Family Systems and Beyond*, New York: Family Sciences Press

Moore, T and West, S (2016), 'Early intervention and the first one thousand days of child development', *Developing Practice*, vol 44

National Stepfamily Resource Center, 'Myths of stepfamilies', www.stepfamilies.info/stepfamily-myths.php

Neuman, M G (1999), *Helping Your Kids Cope with Divorce the Sandcastles Way*, New York: Random House

Nicholson, J M (1999), 'Effects on later adjustment of living in a stepfamily during childhood and adolescence', *Journal of Child Psychology and Psychiatry*, vol 40, no 3, pp 405–16

Nicholson, J M, D'Esposito, F, Lucas, N and Westrupp, E (2014), 'Raising children in single parent families' in Abela, A and Walker, J (eds), *Contemporary Issues in Family Studies: Global Perspectives on Partnerships, Parenting and Support in a Changing World* (1st edition), chapter 12, pp 166–88, Chichester: Wiley-Blackwell

Nicholson, J M, Fergusson, D M and Horwood, L J (1999), 'Effects on later adjustment of living in a stepfamily during childhood and adolescence', *Journal of Child Psychology and Psychiatry*, vol 40, no 3, pp 405–16

Nicholson, J M, Lucas, N and Erbas, B (2013), 'Strengthening the social environment for Australian children: A reply to Parkinson', *Journal of Family Studies*, vol 19, no 3, pp 272–5

Nicholson, J M, Sanders, M R, Halford, W K, Phillips, M and Whitton, S W (2008), 'Prevention and treatment of children's adjustment problems in stepfamilies' in Pryor, J (ed), *The International Handbook of Stepfamilies: Policy and Practice in Legal, Research and Clinical Environments*, pp 485–521, Hoboken: Wiley

Nielsen, L (1999), 'Stepmothers: Why so much stress? A review of the research', *Journal of Divorce and Remarriage*, vol 30, pp 115–48

Nolte, D L and Harris, R (1998), 'Children learn what they live' in *Parenting to Inspire Values*, New York: Workman Publishing Co Inc

Ochiltree, G (1990), *Children in Step-families*, Sydney: Prentice Hall

Pace, G, Shafer, J and Larson, J H (2015), 'Step-parenting issues and relationship quality: The role of clear communication', *Journal of Social Work*, vol 15, no 1, pp 24–44

Papernow, P L (2013), *Surviving and Thriving in Stepfamily Relationships; What Works and What Doesn't*, New York: Routledge

Papernow, P L (2006a), '"Blended family" relationships: Helping people who live in stepfamilies', *Family Therapy Magazine*, May, pp 34–42

Papernow, P L (2006b), 'Stepfamilies clinical update', *Family Therapy Magazine*, vol 5, no 3, pp 34–42

Papernow, P L (1993), *Becoming a Stepfamily: Patterns of Development in Remarriage Families*, New York: Routledge

Papernow, P L (1984), 'The stepfamily cycle: An experimental model of stepfamily development', *Family Relations*, vol 33, pp 355–63

Parrott, L, Parrott, L, Allen, S and Kuna, T (2011), *The Hour That Matters Most: The Surprising Power of the Family Meal*, Carol Stream: Tyndale House Publishers

Patterson, C J and Wainwright, J A (2012), *Adolescents with Same Sex Parents: Findings from the National Longitudinal Study of Adolescent Health*, New York: Oxford University Press

Planitz, J, Feeney, J and Peterson, C (2009), 'Attachment patterns of young adults in stepfamilies and biological families', *Journal of Family Studies* vol 15, no 1, pp 67–81

Pryor, J (ed), *The International Handbook of Stepfamilies: Policy and Practice in Legal, Research and Clinical Environments*, Hoboken: John Wiley

Pryor, J and Rodgers, B (2001), *Children in Changing Families Life after Parental Separation: Understanding Children's Worlds*, Malden: Blackwell

Qu, L, Knight, K and Higgins, D (2016), *Same Sex Couple Families in Australia*, Melbourne: Australian Institute of Family Studies

Qu, L and Weston, R (2008), *Snapshots of Family Relationships*, Melbourne: Australian Institute of Family Studies

Qu, L and Weston, R (2005), *Snapshots of Couple Families with Stepparent–Child Relationships*, Melbourne: Australian Institute of Family Studies

Qu, L, Weston, R, Moloney, L, Kaspiew, R and Dunstan, J (2014), *Post-separation Parenting, Property and Relationship Dynamics after Five Years*, Melbourne: Australian Institute of Family Studies

Robertson, J (2014), *Addressing the Challenges of Stepfamily Life, No 8*, Families Commission, Roy Mackenzie Centre for the Study of Families, New Zealand

Rutter, V (1994), 'Lessons from stepfamilies', *Psychology Today*, vol 27, pp 30–3, 60

Ryan, M, and Claessens, A (2013), 'Associations between family structure changes and children's behaviour problems: The moderating effects of timing and marital birth', *Developmental Psychology*, vol 49, no 7, pp 1219–31

Save the Children (2015), *The Urban Disadvantage: State of World's Mothers*, Fairfield, USA: Save the Children

Save the Children (2015), *State of Australia's Mothers Report*, Carlton: Save the Children

Schmeeckle, M (2007), 'Gender dynamics in stepfamilies: Adult stepchildren's views', *Journal of Marriage and Family*, vol 69, no 1, pp 174–89

Schmeeckle, M, Giarrusso, R, Feng, D and Bengston, V L (2006), 'What makes someone family? Adult children's perceptions of current and former step-parents', *Journal of Marriage and Family*, vol 68, no 3, pp 595–610

Schrodt, P (2006), 'A typological examination of communication competence and mental health in stepchildren', *Communication Monographs*, vol 73, no 3

Seligman, M (2011), *The Optimistic Child*, North Sydney: Penguin Random House

Slattery, M E, Bruce, V, Halford, W K and Nicholson, J M (2011), 'Predicting married and cohabiting couples' futures from their descriptions of stepfamily life', *Journal of Family Psychology*, vol 25, no 4, pp 560–9

Stacey, J (2014), 'Uncoupling marriage and parenting', in McClain, L and Cere, D (eds), *What is Parenthood? Contemporary Debates about the Family*, New York: NYU Press

Stacey, J (1996), *In the Name of the Family: Rethinking Family Values in the Postmodern Age*, Boston: Beacon Press

Stanley, F D (2003), 'It takes a village to raise a child', speech at the Communities in Control Conference, convened by Our Community and Catholic Social Services, Western Australia

Stepfamilies Australia, http://www.stepfamily.org.au/wp-content/uploads/Stepfamilies-grandparent_web.pdf

Stinnett, N and DeFrain, J (1985), *Secrets of Strong Families*, Boston: Little, Brown

Strange, C, Bremner, A, Fisher, C, Howat, P and Wood, L (2015), 'Mothers group participation: Associations with social capital, social support and mental well-being', *Journal of Advanced Nursing*, vol 72, no 1, pp 85–98

Tasker, F (2013), 'Developmental outcomes for children raised by lesbian and gay parents', in McClain, L and Cere, D (eds), *What is Parenthood? Contemporary Debates about the Family*, New York: NYU Press

Visher, E (1979), *Stepfamilies: A Guide to Working with Stepparents and Stepchildren*, New York: Routledge

Visher, E and Visher, J (2014), *Old Loyalties, New Ties*, New York: Routledge

Visher, E and Visher, J (1996), *Therapy with Stepfamilies*, New York: Routledge (Psychology Press)

Visher, E and Visher, J (1995), 'Beyond the nuclear family: Resources and implications for pediatricians', *Pediatric Clinics of North America*, vol 42, no 1, pp 31–43

Visher, E and Visher, J (1991), *How to Win as a Stepfamily*, New York: Routledge

Visher, E and Visher, J (1988), *Old Loyalties, New Ties: Therapeutic Interventions with Stepfamilies*, New York: Brunner/Mazel

Wald, E (1981), *The Remarried Family: Challenge and Promise*, New York: Family Service Association of America

Wallerstein, J and Lewis, J M (2004), 'Second chances—The unexpected legacy of divorce: Report of a 25-year study', *Psychoanalytic Psychology*, vol 21, no 3, pp 353–70

Weaver, S and Coleman, M (2010), 'Caught in the middle: Mothers in stepfamilies', *Journal of Social and Personal Relationships*, vol 27, no 3, pp 305–26

Weston, R, Qu, L and Baxter, J (2015), 'Australian families with children and adolescents', *Australian Family Trends*, no 5, Melbourne: Australian Institute of Family Studies

White, L (1994), 'Growing up with single parents and step parents: Long term effects on family solidarity', *Journal of Marriage and Family*, vol 56, no 4, pp 935–48

White, L and Booth, A (1985), 'The quality and stability of remarriages: The role of stepchildren', *American Sociological Review*, vol 50, no 5, pp 689–98

Whitton, S W, Nicholson, J M and Markman, H J (2008), 'Research on interventions for stepfamily couples: The state of the field', in Pryor, J (ed), *The International Handbook of Stepfamilies: Policy and Practice in Legal, Research and Clinical Environments*, pp 445–84, Hoboken: John Wiley

Wilkins, R (2016), *The Household, Income and Labour Dynamics in Australia Survey: Selected Findings from Waves 1 to 14*, Melbourne: Melbourne Institute, University of Melbourne

Acknowledgements

Bill my beloved, my parents Michael and Quentin, Patricia and Don Edgar, Claire Cartwright, Patricia Papernow, Jan Nicholson, Daryl Higgins, Alan Hayes, Paul Amato, Kathy Mikkelsen, Sally Heath, Cathryn Lea Smith and Louise Adler and to the generous parents, grandparents and children who told me about their family life.

Index